D0030248

On Hope's Wings

On Hope's Wings

MELODY CARLSON

BETHANY HOUSE PUBLISHERS
MINNEAPOLIS, MINNESOTA 55438

On Hope's Wings
Copyright © 1998
Melody Carlson

Cover illustration by Angelo
Cover design by Peter Glöege

All rights reserved. No part of this publication may be reproduced, stored
in a retrieval system, or transmitted in any form or by any means
electronic, mechanical, photocopying, recording or otherwise without the
prior written permission of the publisher and copyright owners.

Published by Bethany House Publishers
A Ministry of Bethany Fellowship, Inc.
11300 Hampshire Avenue South
Minneapolis, Minnesota 55438

Printed in the United States of America.

Library of Congress Cataloging-in-Publication Data

Carlson, Melody.
    On hope's wings / by Melody Carlson.
    p.   cm. — (The Allison chronicles ; 1)
    Summary: In 1948, while her mother is off making yet another movie,
fourteen-year-old Allison O'Brian makes her way from New York to Oregon
to see the grandfather she has never met and to learn what she can about
her supposedly dead father.
    ISBN 1–55661–957-X (pbk.)
    [1. Mothers and daughters—Fiction. 2. Grandfathers—Fiction.
3. Christian life—Fiction.] I. Title. II. Series: Carlson, Melody. Allison
chronicles ; 1.
PZ7.C216637On   1998
[Fic]—dc21   97–33854
                                        CIP
                                        AC

MELODY CARLSON'S many years of experience in working with children have formed the basis for her award-winning career as an author of nearly twenty books, most of them for children and young adults, including *Jessica*, *Benjamin's Box*, *Tupsu*, and *The Ark That Noah Built*. Melody resides with her husband and two teenage sons in Oregon.

Bethany House Publishers
Books by Melody Carlson

——————— ❧ ———————

THE ALLISON CHRONICLES

1. *On Hope's Wings*
2. *Cherished Wish*

❧   ❧   ❧

Awakening Heart
Jessica

9712

To Carol, Erikka,
Heidi, and Bridget,
with love.

1948

One

MISS SNYDER'S OFFICE was as dreary as a dungeon. The dark mahogany walls swallowed most of the light, and the heavy velvet drapes absorbed what little was left. Allison scooted back into the leather chair for the umpteenth time. She hated this stupid chair and the countless minutes wasted in it over the years. The slick seat sloped down as if to torture its occupant by ejecting her slowly to the floor. Meanwhile, the mantel clock steadily counted off precious seconds—time she'd rather spend outdoors with her buddies, not locked up in some musty old office that reeked of furniture polish.

Snatches of conversation and laughter from a softball game invaded the otherwise silent room. Had Patricia struck anyone out? Was their team still ahead? Where was that Miss Snyder, anyway? And what did she want with her on the last day of school? Allison had worked hard to keep her nose clean this final week. She couldn't remember any recent infraction—at least nothing they could pin on her.

The massive door opened and Miss Snyder stepped in. Allison remembered how she'd felt the first time she'd met this headmistress eight years ago. She'd been frightened speechless by the tall, rigid woman who never smiled. But with each passing year, Allison had learned to appreciate the stalwart old maid. Because like it or not, Miss Snyder remained unmovingly predictable. Unlike most of the people in Allison's life.

"I am sorry to have kept you waiting, Miss O'Brian. I was delayed by an inept maintenance man." She switched on her desk lamp, and it illuminated her face with a weird yellow glow, just about the color of Vaseline. "I'll get directly to the point,

Allison. I received a telegram from your mother's secretary to-day. As you are aware, your mother is making one of her motion pictures in Istanbul."

Allison sensed disapproval in Miss Snyder's tone. Frivolous movie stars, especially in these post-war years, were definitely not Miss Snyder's cup of tea. Of course, Allison wasn't proud of her mother's acting career, either, and for many years she had managed to keep it a secret.

Miss Snyder cleared her throat and continued. "I realize you were expecting to join your grandmother in Massachusetts this summer, but now those plans have changed."

Allison frowned. Summer in Cape Cod was one of the high points of her year. She loved the freedom to roam the beaches, to sail, and to explore the quaint little sea towns.

"Your grandmother has taken ill," Miss Snyder said, almost apologetically. She peered at Allison over her wire-rimmed glasses, and her lips softened—almost a smile.

"It figures," Allison muttered under her breath. Grand-mother was always "ill." Why should that ruin this summer? During the war years, Grandmother had been "ill" a lot, but that never stopped Allison's visits. There were plenty of servants at the house, and Allison always stayed well out of Grandmother's way. In fact, it had given her even more freedom to roam around. One time she had spent an entire day hunkered down on the beach, spying on what she was certain must have been a Nazi submarine lurking just off shore.

"Your mother's secretary—" Miss Snyder began again, paus-ing to look at the telegram—"A Miss Lola Stevens has made arrangements for you to attend Wannatonka Summer Camp for Girls." Miss Snyder folded the telegram and nodded as if that solved Allison's problem.

Allison's stomach tightened and she drew in her breath. She had spent one whole summer there two years ago when Grand-mother had closed the house and gone to some resort in Canada. Camp Wannatonka had been the worst experience of Allison's entire life, and she had sworn to never return. The counselors were horribly mean, the food was inedible, and the beds smelled like rotten cabbage. But worse than that, she had been the brunt of some brutal camp jokes initiated by a spiteful older girl Allison had managed to offend the very first day of camp.

"Miss Stevens is sending your things from the city, and you are to leave here Monday morning to arrive at camp in the afternoon." Miss Snyder placed the telegram on her desk and rose slowly from her chair. "Unfortunately, that means you'll have to spend the weekend here on your own since most of the girls will be gone by tomorrow. But I'm sure you'll have a pleasant time at camp, Allison."

No, I won't, Allison thought, gritting her teeth in anger. She forced herself to smile and thank Miss Snyder.

Outside, Allison lost all interest in the softball game. She sat on an old wooden bench and buried her head in her hands. She pressed her cold fingers across her eyes—she would not cry. No, that was a childish way to act. She needed to think. Like Winston Churchill had said during the war, "The only thing to fear is fear itself." She couldn't be afraid of anything. She would figure a way out of Camp Wannatonka. If only she had some place to hide out for the next few months. . . .

The June sun felt warm on her back, promising a summer of fun that she knew it could not deliver. She looked up to see the string of expensive, shiny cars already lining the long drive. They were here to pick up her classmates and take them home for their summer break. Some were manned by chauffeurs, others with real, live parents. It seemed everyone but Allison was going home. It just wasn't fair!

Home . . . Where was her home, anyway? The Cape, where Grandmother feigned sickness to keep her away? Here at Oakmont, the girls' boarding school where she had spent most of her life? Or her mother's penthouse in New York City, where she stayed for an occasional weekend or holiday when it was convenient? Did she really belong anywhere? Allison thought again of her mother's vacated penthouse. It could be a handy hideaway—and she did have a key.

"Hey, Al, what'cha up to?" Patricia dashed across the grounds to join Allison, her long black braids flapping behind her. "We lost the game without you, kiddo! I just cannot pitch like you, Al. You've definitely got the magic arm. Then stupid ol' Cynthia Merrick struck me out—she thought she was pretty snazzy, too!" Allison didn't even look up.

"Hey, Al, what's wrong? Why so glum, chum?" Patricia peered at Allison with sympathy.

"Oh, Trish, it's just horrible!" Allison exploded. "My grand-mother, as usual, claims she's sick, so they're shipping me off to that horrible Camp Wannatonka! I just can't take another summer there!"

"Oh, Al, you told me all about that place! It sounded like a real nightmare! But you never know, maybe it'll be better this time."

Allison shook her head. "I doubt that, Trish. Besides, it's a chance I refuse to take!" She glanced across the wide green lawn. Miss Snyder had just left the administration offices and was now walking purposefully toward the dining hall.

"Trish, I have this crazy idea," Allison said, keeping one eye on Miss Snyder as she pulled Patricia to her feet. "Will you help me?" They'd been cohorts since first grade, and Allison knew she could count on her best friend. She explained her plan as they slipped into the administration building.

"You keep watch," Allison whispered as they tiptoed down the deserted hallway. "Tap twice on the door if anyone comes. Then beat it—okay? Otherwise, just return my signal if the coast is clear." Patricia winked and Allison slipped into Miss Snyder's office.

There on the desk lay the yellow telegram. Allison quickly copied the camp's address and returned the telegram to the exact spot. The clock seemed louder than usual as Allison slid open a drawer of Miss Snyder's bulky wooden file cabinet. She looked through the M section first, since her mother's name was Marsha Madison. But Allison's file wasn't there. After a desperate search she finally found it under her own name: Allison Mercury O'Brian. She wondered again why her father had chosen to endow her with such a strange middle name. A middle name that had, in fact, brought its own share of troubles.

Allison found an old admission form with her mother's signature on it. She stuffed it into her shirt, then tapped out her "all done" signal to Patricia and held her breath. The signal was returned, and they streaked back to their room suppressing giggles mixed with terror and triumph. Allison went right to work on Patricia's upright typewriter.

"Al, I've gotta hand it to you. You've got more nerve than a bandit at a necktie party."

Allison grinned at her friend with pride and continued to peck on the typewriter. "How does this sound?" Allison read the counterfeit letter. " 'Wannatonka Summer Camp: Dear Camp Director. Due to unforeseen circumstances I have decided to have my daughter, Allison O'Brian, stay with her grandmother in Massachusetts this summer. I apologize for any inconvenience. Please keep my payment as a donation to your fine and upstanding camp. Sincerely, Marsha Madison.' " Allison practiced her mother's scrawled signature over and over until she had it nearly perfect.

"You're too much, Al! And the part about a donation is brilliant. But now what will you do? Where will you stay if you're not at camp?"

"Marsha Madison's New York penthouse," she stated. "I have my own key, you know." Allison licked the envelope and grinned.

"All by yourself?" Patricia exclaimed, eyes wide.

Allison nodded. "Why not? They all treat me like I don't exist anyway. So I'll just not exist in New York for the summer. Who knows, it might even be fun!"

With the letter complete, they headed for dinner. Allison tried not to dance as she entered the dining hall. Just the idea of what she was about to pull off made her light-headed.

"I'll just drop this in the mail," she announced nonchalantly to Miss Snyder as she slipped the letter into the postbox, right under the headmistress's long, skinny nose. Patricia exploded into a fit of laughter, and Allison gently dug her elbow into her friend's ribs. She couldn't afford to push her luck too far.

Two

THE EVACUATED DORM was dark and strangely silent. Allison lay awake in her bed too excited to sleep. She couldn't believe what she was about to do. She'd cooked up some wild schemes in her time, but this one beat them all. Still, why should she worry? She had nothing to lose. Her mother was worlds away—in more ways than miles. In fact, "mother" was a contradiction in terms. Marsha, as she insisted Allison call her, was hardly what anyone would consider a fine example of motherhood. Allison couldn't even recall if she'd ever played a mother in any of her movie pictures.

Allison searched her mind to try to recapture her first memory of Marsha. Allison had been around three, maybe four. She had been living at Grandmother Madison's estate on the Cape, the very same house that Marsha had grown up in. One day, Grandmother had sternly instructed Allison's nanny to get Allison out from under foot. Dear Nanny Jane had obliged, taking Allison down to the garden for one of her special tea parties. They would take Allison's favorite rag doll and teddy bear, a set of tiny dishes, and even real tea.

But on this particular day, a strange woman approached them. At first Allison had thought the woman was very beautiful, but when she got closer Allison wasn't so sure. The woman's hair was blacker than Nanny's polished shoes, and her lips were red like blood. Allison had thought she looked like the wicked queen in the movie *Snow White* that Nanny Jane had taken her to see. Allison remembered hiding behind Nanny Jane's crisp starched apron. It had protected her like a bright white canopy, and the sun shone through and smelled just like summer.

Allison tossed sleeplessly in her bed, trying to shut down her mind and the memories she had induced, but flashes of Marsha kept coming, taunting her. She remembered her fifth birthday when Marsha had come once again to the Madison estate, only this time Allison had received some warning. Nanny Jane had explained that the strange woman was actually Allison's mother, and Allison should be polite and courteous to her. The woman wore a long fur piece with the head of an animal still attached, and Allison had worried that the sharp-nosed critter might also have sharp teeth. Her mother had brought with her a large box wrapped in shiny gold foil and tied with a big pink bow. Allison had shyly accepted the gift, keeping a wary eye on the frightening animal the whole while.

"Her hair is red . . . just like *his*," the woman said to Grandmother Madison, speaking as if Allison's ears were stuffed with cotton. "And freckles, too! You almost wouldn't think she was truly *my* daughter. Has he attempted to see her lately?"

Allison stared blankly into the glassy blue eyes of the strange porcelain doll without even removing her from the gift box. The fancy doll wore a stiff pink lacy dress, and fat blond curls hung like sausages on each side of her round pink cheeks.

"He has tried see her, but so far we've managed to keep him at bay," Grandmother Madison had answered in her haughty voice. Allison could never figure out why Grandmother spoke in such an exaggerated tone. Why would anyone want to sound like that?

Grandmother Madison adjusted her elegant spectacles, cleared her throat, and continued. "And when, may I ask, do you intend to get that divorce? I say the sooner the better." Allison hadn't understood all they'd said, but she'd known that somehow it concerned her, too.

"Do I have a daddy?" Allison had asked Nanny Jane that evening at bedtime.

"Certainly, darling. Everyone has a father." Nanny Jane turned her face away. "Would you like to sleep with your new dolly tonight?"

Allison shook her head—she did not want that thing in her bed. Instead, she cuddled up to her old, familiar teddy.

Their bedtime ritual was always the same. Nanny Jane sat by her bed and together they recited the Lord's Prayer. Allison loved how the *r*'s rolled off Nanny Jane's tongue when she said, "Our Father which art in heaven . . ." Nanny Jane had told Allison about her homeland in Scotland, an ancient, rocky island far, far away, with castles, clans, and bagpipes. Allison thought it must be a wonderful place because of the tales Nanny Jane told. Then Nanny Jane would sing an old Scottish lullaby from her rocker by the window. Allison would watch her sitting and knitting by the soft glow of the nursery lamp until her sleepy eyes would refuse to stay open.

Allison turned again on her squeaky dorm bed. "I've got to get some sleep," she muttered. Tomorrow she would need all her wits in order to pull off her daring escape.

இஒ   இஒ   இஒ

The sun rose without mercy for Allison's restless night. As she moved about her room, her footsteps echoed in the empty dormitory. The last of the girls had left yesterday. She'd been sad to tell her friends good-bye. Patricia had even offered to beg her parents to allow Allison to spend the latter half of the summer with them when they returned from their vacation to Yellowstone Park. They'd both promised to write.

Allison joined Miss Snyder for breakfast in the large, vacant dining hall. It was strange with just the two of them. Allison used great self-control to keep from wolfing down her eggs. She didn't want to draw unwanted attention, and she couldn't risk

Miss Snyder's suspicion or inquisitive comments.

After breakfast Miss Snyder's chauffeur drove Allison to the train station. He opened the door and reached for her bag.

"No need for that," she assured him, wrestling the bag from his bony grip. "Now, you just be on your way. Thank you." She smiled brightly and watched his mustache twitch in surprise, but fortunately he climbed back into the big car. She waited until he drove out of sight, then rushed to the ticket counter. A round man in a pillbox hat asked if he could assist her.

"Oh yes, I'm in a terrible dither, sir. My mother just tele-grammed from New York City. My father has taken seriously ill, and I must exchange my ticket to Wannatonka for New York City. Can you please help me?" She lifted her brows in her most beguiling look.

"Dear me, let me see . . . I think I can, miss. Yes, I've got one on the noon train!" He looked at his watch. "Are you ready?" She nodded and thanked him, and the next thing she knew she was on her way.

She had stayed in New York only a few times before, her most recent visit last Christmas. Marsha had been forced to take her, since Grandmother Madison had been "ill"—although Allison had overheard Marsha mention a big party at Grand-mother's estate during the holidays. Allison always pretended not to be overly impressed by Marsha's fancy penthouse. It was, after all, just a part of the package deal that came with Marsha's latest husband, Stanley. He was husband number three on the rapidly growing list and the oldest one so far.

Marsha never wanted people to know that Allison was her daughter, and therefore she demanded that Allison play the role of her younger sister. Not only that, Allison was expected to col-laborate on Marsha's amazing new age, twenty-six, which was exactly half that of Stanley's. Marsha said this was for the sake of her acting career. It seemed like a silly game, but Allison played along. And somehow Marsha's deceptions made it easier for Allison to create her own lies now. If Marsha could get away with it, why shouldn't she?

She watched as the serene countryside of upstate New York slowly melded into suburbs. Before long, the buildings became denser, then taller. Suddenly, she wondered how she would survive an entire summer of city life. Already she felt the beginnings of claustrophobia. She checked her billfold for money again. Somehow seeing the bills neatly lined up was reassuring to her. It was allowance money that Marsha had sent to Allison each month. It was always much more than Allison needed, and she usually just stashed it away in her sock drawer. It sure would come in handy now.

The train pulled into Grand Central Station, and Allison grabbed her one small bag and waited nearly an hour for a taxi. At last she climbed in wearily and wondered if she had made a serious mistake. New York City was a very big place!

"What's a young'un like you doing out on her own?" asked the grisly old taxi driver.

"Well, my folks would've met me from boarding school, but you see, my mom's having a baby and my daddy had to get her to the hospital this morning. I'm on my way to stay with my grandmother." She marveled at how easily that whopper rolled off her tongue.

"Well, congratulations, young lady. That's quite an event!"

Allison sighed and leaned back. She was getting pretty good at this.

The cabby wished her family well as she climbed out in front of the gleaming high rise. The doorman eyed her curiously, and she lowered her head and scurried past his open door. His suspicion seemed to follow her across the polished lobby floor.

The elevator soared to the seventeenth floor and, as usual, made her stomach sink and her head spin. She staggered down the carpeted hall and began the search for the right apartment. All the doors looked exactly the same. Finally at the end of the hall, Allison stopped in front of a glossy red door—number 1748. She knew that Stanley had accompanied Marsha to Istanbul, but suddenly she wondered if someone else could possibly be inside. What about the maid? What if the locks had been changed? Or what if it was the wrong apartment number? She held her breath, slipped in the key, and turned—it worked!

Not knowing what to expect, Allison cautiously opened the door. It was dark and the blinds were down. Footsteps sounded behind her in the hallway, and she quickly stepped inside and shut the door behind her. Her heart pounded with anticipation as she fumbled for the light switch. The furnishings were covered in ghostly white shrouds with no sign of occupants.

Zipping through the apartment, she jerked open shades, flipped on more lights, and undraped the furniture. This was great! She flicked on the radio and collapsed on Marsha's enormous burgundy couch. Rich tones of Duke Ellington floated through the room, and she absently scanned one of Marsha's fashion magazines. This sudden new freedom was almost overwhelming—what should she do next?

Food! Would there be anything to eat? Allison went to the refrigerator—empty. A few staples in the cupboards, but certainly not enough to last the summer. Oh well, she'd think about that later. She opened a tin of sardines and ate them on soda crackers. A tiny can of fruit cocktail and some shortbread made a dessert that she topped off with tea.

Next she explored the bookshelf for reading material. Although Marsha had never been much of a reader, it appeared Stanley enjoyed a good book because there were several to choose from. She picked an F. Scott Fitzgerald novel. Miss Snyder wouldn't approve, but then Miss Snyder would hardly approve of any of this. Allison soon became lost in the steamy novel.

When she finally glanced at the clock, it was after nine and dark outside—at least as dark as it gets in the Big Apple from the seventeenth floor. The incredible New York skyline looked like a glittering fairyland—dazzling, spectacular, and almost enticing. What was it really like down there? Did a fourteen-year-old dare venture out after dark?

Allison chided herself—there was still so much to explore in the penthouse. She wandered aimlessly through the elegant rooms. Stanley had a separate bedroom connected to Marsha's with a two-way locking door. His room was dark and serious-looking, and it smelled faintly of stale cigars. In Marsha's luxurious bedroom, Allison freely snooped. She started by opening a set of gilded double doors to discover another miniature room, which was actually an enormous closet filled with rows of dresses and gowns, suits and coats, stacks of sweaters, and dozens and dozens of shoes. It reminded her of a department store. How could one woman ever begin to wear all this stuff?

The closet was saturated with the familiar scent of Marsha's overpowering perfume. That smell had always given Allison a headache and made her stomach queasy, and tonight it was no different. She flopped across Marsha's big bed and analyzed this bedroom with perplexity. Just who was this woman who lived here, anyway? This famous Marsha Madison—this stranger. How was it that she could really be Allison's mother?

Three

ALLISON SAT ON her mother's bed and smoothed her hand over the mauve satin bedspread. She studied the roses on the wallpaper. They were peculiar flowers outlined in black, cold and rigid as if chiseled from stone. They climbed up the wall to an ornate molding that outlined the high ceiling. The huge chandelier, with its long slivers of crystal, hung menacingly over the gilded four-poster bed. It looked like it would kill her if it fell. Some might have called Marsha's bedroom gorgeous, but Allison thought it was garish and overdone—a lot like her mother.

For the first time in her life, Allison had a compelling interest in this woman who'd conceived her. But it was almost a morbid curiosity, like the time she and Patricia found the dead cow in Warner Greeley's field. The smell was sickening and they knew they should leave it alone, but they couldn't resist poking its bloated carcass with a stick. She shuddered as she remembered the results.

Allison examined her mother's dressing table with its many fancy bottles of perfume, makeup, combs, and creams. So much was still here that she wondered if Marsha had taken anything to Istanbul. She twisted open an engraved silver lipstick tube. It was an orangish shade, not the deep scarlet Marsha usually wore. Allison pretended to apply some lipstick, making the same face Marsha did, but the massive mirror took her by surprise and she laid down the tube. She wasn't used to seeing her entire reflection at once. Back in the dormitory they had two tiny square mirrors for twenty girls to fight over, but she rarely bothered. She had little use for primping. Marsha's acidic remarks about her hair and freckles had imprinted themselves in her brain.

She studied her reflection. Her wavy red hair was divided in two straggly braids that never hung straight. Her skin was too pale and freckled, and her eyes seemed oversized for her face. Nanny had said they were hazel eyes that changed like the sea. Allison stared but didn't see any changes. Just flecks of blue and green and brown, almost like someone couldn't decide which color to use. Her blue school uniform did nothing to enhance her appearance, either. Marsha may have been right about her looks, but Allison knew there was more to life than being pretty. After all, no one at school could pitch as well or run as fast as she could.

Out of the corner of her eye she spotted an old photograph of Marsha. Allison moved over to the chest of drawers where it stood and picked it up in amazement. She'd never seen it before. It was her mother and yet it wasn't. She looked different. She was younger and strangely void of makeup. Allison slipped the photo from the frame and examined the back. *Marsha, 18* was all it said. When Allison was asked, she never described her mother as beautiful. Maybe glamorous, elegant, or sophisticated, but in this photo Marsha did look beautiful. Allison stretched across Marsha's wide bed and stared into the photo as if some secret message might be hidden there.

She knew her mother had been only eighteen when she first came to New York to study drama. Nanny Jane had told Allison all about it. Acting was Marsha's passion—her only dream. Her parents strongly opposed the idea at first, but they finally gave in. Marsha usually got what she wanted. It was the heart of the depression then, but the Madison family's wealth was barely affected. According to Nanny Jane, Marsha's parents sent her a generous monthly allowance, quite an advantage for a struggling young actress. They paid for her acting lessons and introduced her to their "connections."

Somewhere along the line, Marsha hooked up with James O'Brian, an aspiring and talented artist. Nanny Jane had said he was a handsome young man, tall and straight, with clear eyes that reminded her of the ocean. Actress and artist married, and what might have been a storybook ending went against Marsha's parents' wishes. The allowance was terminated. That's about all Nanny had said.

Allison returned the photo to the dresser and slid open the top drawer. She knew she shouldn't snoop, but she was fed up with all the mystery in her life. She was tired of unanswered questions.

There was nothing of particular interest in the first few drawers, just lacy lingerie and silk stockings. Finally, buried beneath some negligees in the bottom drawer, she found what looked like a small, plush jewelry box. It was covered in faded blue velveteen and worn on the corners. It could've come from Woolworth's and stood out like a beggar amidst Marsha's costly things.

Allison opened it slowly, and tinkling music box tones escaped. She snapped it shut, then remembered she was alone. Opening it again, she listened to the sad melody of *Swan Lake* and puzzled over the odd contents. A bent spoon, ticket stubs, a faded rose, an old, frayed ribbon, and a key. Old mementos—fragmented pieces of a fragmented life. Yet Allison felt certain they related to her father and an earlier time.

The stubs were dated in the war years. Allison remembered asking Marsha about her father during that time. Marsha had answered stonily, "He's overseas—in the war."

Later Nanny Jane had confirmed it. "That's what I heard, too, darling. Now each night when you say your prayers, you must say a special one for him. War is a horrible thing. . . ." Nanny's sweet old face had looked sad and gray. She'd lost her only son in the first big war. That was long ago, before she'd come overseas to be Marsha's nanny. Allison never could imagine Marsha as a little girl, let alone with her Nanny Jane. She closed the music box and returned it to the drawer.

In Marsha's bathroom, the huge marble tub seemed to beckon her. Allison turned on the water, then dumped in a generous amount of French bubble bath. This would be a treat! She went to the spare bedroom, supposedly "her room," though it never felt like it, and peered into "her" closet. Empty! Where were her clothes? Did Marsha have everything sent to Wannatonka? She pulled open a bureau drawer—also empty. All she possessed were the clothes on her back! How could she traipse around New York City in her school uniform all summer? That would sure draw some attention—just what she didn't need.

Allison dashed back to the bathroom in the nick of time and shut off the gold-plated faucet. Bubbles cascaded down the sides of the tub and onto the shiny black tiles. She giggled mischievously. This was a luxury she seldom enjoyed. The shower room at school was drafty and noisy with a cold cement floor. She sank slowly into the suds, careful not to splash the water. "Ahh," she sighed, "I suppose I could get used to this. . . ."

She dried off on Marsha's thick Egyptian towels, creamed, powdered, and pampered herself, then slipped into a peach satin robe that hung on the bathroom door. She passed Marsha's full-length mirror and stared in disbelief. Her damp hair curled loosely around her shoulders, and her cheeks were pink from her bath. The clingy robe exposed some new feminine curves. This didn't look like the Allison she knew. Rummaging through Marsha's drawers, she searched fruitlessly for a warm nightie. All she found were silk, lace, and satin—hardly what she considered warm and cozy.

After fixing herself another cup of tea, Allison was ready to call it a night. She headed for her room, which felt cold and uninviting. The starched white bedspread was so stiff it crackled when she sat on it. She figured Marsha had decorated this room purposely to discourage visitors from overstaying. Well,

Allison intended to make herself at home this time.

She marched into Marsha's spacious bedroom and threw back the covers on the oversized bed. "It figures," she laughed. "Satin sheets!" She slid in, sipped her steaming tea, and recovered her place in the book. Finally her eyes refused to focus, and the silky sheets absorbed her last shred of strength.

❦   ❦   ❦

Warm morning sunlight filtered through the filmy lace curtains. Allison stretched luxuriantly, but her stomach rumbled discontent. "I've got to get some real food, and that means leaving this apartment." She remembered the doorman's suspicious glance. He was probably unaccustomed to uniformed schoolgirls in his highfaluting high rise. How could she slip past him without notice?

She looked at Marsha's closet and remembered Stanley's comment at Christmas, *"By golly, Marsha, your baby sister is as tall as you!"*

"That's it! I'll become a grown-up!" Allison scrambled out of bed and rummaged through the closet. She'd need just the right outfit. It had to be convincing—not too old or sophisticated. Most of Marsha's clothes looked like they belonged on a movie set with their feathers, sequins, and fur. At last Allison tossed a few possibilities out on the bed. She tried them on, and miraculously they fit! A little loose in spots, but nothing obvious. Now what about shoes? Would she be so lucky? She slipped her silk-stockinged foot into a green suede pump. Perfect! She felt almost like Cinderella.

Allison stood before the full-length mirror. The color and line of the celery green linen suit were perfect for her. She turned this way and that, admiring the outfit. The pendulum jacket jutted out right above the hips, but something was wrong. Her hair! It was nothing like the coiffures she'd seen in Marsha's fashion magazines.

After several hopeless attempts with Marsha's fancy combs and pins, she gave up. A hat might help. She searched several hat boxes before she discovered the perfect moss green hat. Better, but still not quite right. If she wanted to pass for a sophisticated young woman, she needed a bit of makeup. She applied a little of the orangish lipstick and a touch of rouge. She stared at the young woman in the mirror and smiled at the transformation. If only Patricia were here, wouldn't they have fun?

Now for some jewelry. She opened Marsha's big rosewood jewelry box. It contained only costume and inexpensive pieces. Allison selected a mother-of-pearl pin and matching bracelet. As she put them on, the familiarity hit her. She'd bought them for Marsha a few summers ago on the Cape. For no special reason she'd wanted to do something daughterly. Marsha had smiled sweetly and thanked her, but Allison felt certain she'd never worn them.

Allison slipped on a pair of smooth white gloves—she knew ladies always wore gloves in the city. She tucked her money into a green suede purse and headed out the door. As she locked the door behind her she noticed the place was a mess, but she'd deal with it later.

After she stepped off the elevator in the lobby, the doorman tipped his hat and smiled as he opened the door. "Morning, miss," he said politely. She felt certain he didn't recognize her as yesterday's schoolgirl. She squared her shoulders and walked by with fresh confidence. This was terrific! But now which way to go?

She looked down the street. A cabby called out, "Need a taxi, miss?"

She stumbled into the yellow and black cab, balancing her hat with one hand. This might take some work. It was like playing a role—creating a character and carrying it off.

"Excuse me, sir," she said politely, then wondered if a lady should call a cabby "sir." "Can you drive me to a nice restaurant?

I'm not very familiar with New York City." He drove her to Fifth Avenue and stopped in front of the elegant Grand Hotel. She paid him and climbed out, this time with more grace.

Inside, she sat by a bubbling fountain and scanned the breakfast menu. She selected Eggs Benedict, grapefruit, and coffee. It sounded like a mature sort of breakfast to order. She didn't normally drink coffee, but with sugar and cream it proved tasty and seemed more grown-up than tea. At a nearby table an older gentleman laughed loudly with a smiling young lady— probably his daughter. Allison wondered what her own father might have been like. Surely not like that portly man with the shiny bald head. No, her father would have been tall and handsome. . . .

She remembered the day Marsha had told her that her father was dead. It was the end of October and the trees were golden. Allison had been eight and in her second year at Oakmont when Marsha visited on Parents' Day—the only year she came. Just before Marsha climbed back into her chauffeured limousine she informed Allison of her father's death. Said he'd been killed in the war—just like that. Allison cried for several days. She'd never really known him, but a corner of her heart grew cold and empty just the same.

Allison left a dollar on the table for a tip just as she'd seen Marsha do. Her head grew hot and itchy beneath the contemptible hat, but she didn't dare remove it for her hair was a sight. As she strolled down the sidewalk, she noticed an exclusive-looking beauty salon and decided to investigate.

"May I help you?" asked a tall brunette woman with dangling silver earrings.

"Yes, I'd like my hair done," Allison stated. She'd never been inside a beauty parlor. Nanny Jane had always trimmed her bangs when she was little, and Allison had since taken over after that.

"Do you have an appointment?" The earrings jingled as she spoke.

"Well . . . no," Allison stammered. "You see, I'm from out of town, and I . . . uh . . . I needed—"

"Normally we don't take walk-ins, but I do have a cancellation at one. Will that work?"

"That'll be fine." Allison wondered what she'd do for the next three hours.

"Name?"

Allison thought for a moment. "Sheila—" she blurted. Her eyes darted around the store, and she saw a sign behind the counter for LaVelle hair cream. "Sheila LaVelle," she stated. The brunette eyed her with interest. Allison smiled and felt like an idiot. *What a dumb thing to say*, she thought.

"Could you please tell me the way to Macy's department store?" Allison asked, hoping to conceal her blunder.

"A few blocks that way and two doors down," pointed the receptionist. Allison impressed the directions in her memory and left. Maybe she wouldn't return. Sheila LaVelle—oh brother!

Macy's was as enormous as she remembered but not nearly so busy. She'd gone Christmas shopping there with Stanley last December. He'd picked up dozens of expensive trifles for his new wife. Of course, Marsha's real present had been a full-length silver fox coat.

Allison passed the long glass case of the perfume counter. Pretty boxes and cut-glass bottles lined the shelves, and a pleasant aroma tantalized her nose. It was nothing like Marsha's heavy perfume. This fragrance was light and airy, almost like a spring meadow.

"May I help you?" asked a perky blonde. She wore a tight sweater and a little too much lipstick, but her smile seemed genuine.

"Something smells wonderful. Can you tell me what it is?" Allison asked.

The clerk's eyes lit up. "Well, I just sampled a little of this new perfume," she whispered confidentially. "It came in from Paris yesterday—the first we've gotten from this company since the war. It's called *Fleur des Champ*, or flowers of the field." She held up her wrist for Allison to smell.

"Luscious," breathed Allison. "I'll take some." The price was surprising, but Allison had never purchased perfume before.

"Have a good day," said the cashier with a bright smile as she handed Allison the package.

Allison rode the escalator to the top of the store and down again. There was so much to see, she didn't know where to begin. She stopped on the fourth floor. What she really needed was a warm nightgown. Marsha's flimsy things were for the birds. She selected a thick flannel with tiny pink rosebuds.

Glancing at her watch, she was dismayed to find it was only half past eleven and already she felt ravenous. That light breakfast just hadn't cut it. Maybe an early lunch would help. In Macy's restaurant she quickly devoured a BLT, then lingered over tea. Nanny Jane had always made a good BLT. Often she used lettuce and tomatoes straight from her tiny victory garden.

After Allison started school at Oakmont, she'd always looked forward to returning to the Cape for summers and holidays. Occasionally Marsha stopped by in between productions, but Nanny Jane was the one Allison looked forward to seeing. Nanny Jane had a rented cottage that overlooked the sea and provided a haven for Allison. Together they combed the beach, baked cookies, and had tea out on the screened sun porch. Nanny knit hundreds of woolen socks for soldiers during the war, and Allison helped. She wondered if perhaps her father had worn a pair of her socks before he died. . . .

With a deep sigh, Allison finished her tea and paid the bill. It was then that she noticed her billfold getting thinner. "Excuse me, miss," she inquired of the blonde on her way out. "Do you happen to know where I could pick up a few food items nearby?"

"Well, there's a specialty food store down the street. I can't afford to shop there myself, but I've heard they have quite an interesting selection." The blonde patted her sleek hair in place and smiled prettily.

The shop, a kind of a gourmet delicatessen, was easy to find. Allison chose some tangerines, a petite loaf of bread, a small tin of smoked salmon, and another of Danish ham. On top of these she placed a round of Gouda cheese coated in red wax and a wedge of Swiss. *Groceries aren't cheap*, she thought as the woman totaled the bill.

Since it was now almost one, she placed her parcels in a large shopping bag and returned to the salon. Did she really want to do this? But she couldn't bear to wear hats all summer, and her long hair looked so juvenile. They weren't ready for her appointment, so she flipped through a magazine. There in a swimsuit ad was just the hair she wanted. It looked kind of like the blond cashier's. Smooth and silky and turned under at the shoulders, with short bangs in front.

"Miss LaVelle," the brunette called. "Sheila LaVelle?" she repeated impatiently and tapped Allison on the shoulder.

"Oh yes," Allison answered. "I was . . . uh . . . just daydreaming, I guess." She smiled her most charming smile and this time the brunette returned it.

"This is Helen. She'll take care of you, Miss LaVelle."

The beautician wore a pink smock that blended with her face, and she tied a matching pink cape over Allison's shoulders. Everything in the salon seemed to be the color of cotton candy.

"Well, what can I do for you today, honey?" Helen asked warmly. She didn't look like a beautician. Instead, she had that motherly look, sort of like an advertisement for baking powder.

Allison could just picture her with a rolling pin and flour on the tip of her nose.

Allison showed Helen the magazine. "I'd like my hair just like this."

"You mean this cut and style?"

"Yes, and that color, too," Allison stated boldly. She hadn't really intended to change her hair color, but why not? Marsha's disdainful words echoed through her mind again. *"Her hair's red, just like his."*

Helen studied the photo and gently fingered Allison's long curls. She looked at Allison and frowned. "How old are you, honey?" she asked.

"I'm almost eighteen."

"Hmm." Helen pursed her lips. "Well, honey, it's none of my business, but I can't understand why you want to get rid of that beautiful color. Why, just yesterday Madeline Witherspoon was in here—wanted me to color her hair this very shade. And she's a very tasteful and lovely young debutante."

Allison considered this. No one had ever called her hair beautiful before. Something about Helen made Allison trust her. "Okay. How about just the cut and style?"

Helen smiled. "I think we can do that." After washing, cutting, curling, and what felt like hours under the hair dryer, Helen finally styled her hair. "Now, if you just put in a few curlers on the ends at night like this," Helen explained, "it'll be real easy to keep up."

"Oh, thank you so much, Helen. I just love it!" Allison beamed into the big mirror before her.

"Well, honey, I'm sure glad. Now, don't you ever think about changing that beautiful color, understand?"

Allison nodded, paid the cashier, and carried her hat out the door. She knew the Grand Hotel served afternoon tea, and once again she felt half starved. A young man in a pinstriped suit tipped his hat as she entered the hotel restaurant. She blushed and looked the other way. Masculine attention was new to her. She wasn't sure whether she liked it or not. It might take some getting used to.

The specialty of the afternoon was cream caramel custard. She hadn't tasted any since before Nanny died. She swallowed each bite over a large lump in her throat and reminisced over her last afternoon with Nanny Jane.

They'd sat in Nanny's sun porch overlooking the cliffs by the sea. It was only last fall—Labor Day weekend. If Allison had known it was the last time she'd see Nanny . . . oh, the things she'd have said. "I love you." "Thank you for all you've done for me." "Thanks for all the care packages you've sent me at school, full of cookies and mittens and packed with love. . . ." But Nanny was gone, and this time an even larger vacuum had entered Allison's heart.

What was it Nanny had said that day? Allison racked her memory. Something like, *"Allison, you're almost a woman now, and you'll have to make your own choices in this world. You'll have to learn to depend on yourself and create your own identity. Separate from the rest of them."*

What had she meant? Allison wondered. *What identity? Separate from what?* Suddenly, Allison saw herself in a whole new light. Here she sat in a fancy New York restaurant dressed in her mother's clothes, the woman she disdained more than any other. Had she already become like Marsha?

The thought turned her stomach. No, this was just a masquerade—a silly game. Allison tried to convince herself, but did she believe it?

Four

BACK AT THE APARTMENT, Allison noticed a small pile of mail inside the front door. It seemed a little odd that Marsha still had her mail delivered while she was gone, but Allison just left it on the floor. Wouldn't Marsha be furious to find her apartment like this? Well, it served her right for trying to ship Allison off to that awful camp!

Allison kicked off the platform shoes in relief, stashed her food rations away, and put some Glenn Miller records on the phonograph. The apartment felt so stuffy she opened a window. The air outside wasn't exactly springtime fresh, but it helped a little. She heard sounds of rush-hour traffic and automobile horns far below. She imagined a tired dad going home to his wife and kids in the suburbs. A world about as familiar to her as Mars or, better yet, Mercury, like her middle name. She remembered how Marsha had gotten irritated when Allison asked about that name.

"It was your father's silly idea," Marsha had stated, giving Allison that don't-bring-it-up-again look.

"I wonder if Marsha has any comfortable clothes?" Allison questioned out loud. Her voice sounded strange in the empty apartment. She dug deep in Marsha's fathomless closet and discovered what must have been the sportswear section, and apparently it had been used very little. She found sweaters, jerseys, trousers, shorts, even several bathing suits. *Well, Lola's good for something*, Allison thought. She knew that Lola, her mother's secretary, did most of Marsha's shopping, and it was plain to see these somewhat practical clothes had not been picked out by Marsha.

Allison slipped into a pair of tan rayon pleated pants and pulled a squash-colored jersey over her head. "Ah, much better," she declared. Allison felt frazzled from her day, yet she hadn't accomplished much. She curled up on the couch to the sweet strains of Glenn Miller and opened her nearly finished novel, wondering if Stanley's books would last her the summer.

❧   ❧   ❧

A loud ringing startled her awake. It was pitch black. Where was she? The phone rang again. Oh yes, now she remembered—Marsha's apartment. The telephone—should she answer it? It rang and rang. Allison remained frozen on the couch, as if the other party would hear her if she moved. At last the ringing stopped, and she fumbled for the lights. Who could be calling? Marsha's friends would know she was working on location.

Allison yawned, wondering how long she had slept. It was after ten, so she fixed herself a late-night supper with her new groceries. She had better make her food last as long as possible because her money seemed to be dwindling fast. She pulled out her billfold and counted her cash.

"Forty-nine dollars and sixty-eight cents!" she exclaimed in disbelief. How much had she spent? Her money surely wouldn't last at the rate she'd spent it today. Maybe Marsha had some money around the apartment. She'd think about that tomorrow. Besides, there was always Patricia and Vermont. Maybe she could visit her later in the summer.

❧   ❧   ❧

The next morning a noise at the front door startled her awake. Who could it be? A burglar? Marsha? A burglar might be the safer of the two, considering the condition of the apartment right now. Was someone in the house? Clutching the covers to her chin, Allison listened. Silence. She snatched the robe and crept into the hallway. Everything appeared to be fine, except perhaps the mail stack had grown. "Oh, just the mailman," she sighed in relief. "But if Marsha still has her mail delivered, why wasn't there any mail here on Monday?" she pondered out loud.

She walked over to the mail pile and scratched her head. Now, where did Marsha normally keep her letters and bills? In the corner of the expansive living room, Allison spotted the tall, hand-carved rosewood secretary. Of course! Allison pulled open the writing desk and there lay several neat stacks of mail. Who had been sorting Marsha's mail? Next to the stack was a list written in Marsha's scrawled handwriting.

Lola,
1- *Please sort and forward any important mail.*
2- *Water the rubber plant weekly.*
3- *Clean the refrigerator.*
4- *Call my mother every few days and let her know if anything's wrong.*
5- *Write to Allison at camp at least twice a month.*

Thanks,
Miss Madison

"Thanks to you, too, Miss Madison," Allison said sarcastically. "How nice of you to tell your secretary to write to your own daughter! Such a warm and personal gesture!" She threw down the note in disgust and slammed the secretary shut so hard the leaded glass windows rattled above.

Allison stomped into the kitchen and filled the teakettle, then angrily sliced some bread for toast. The nerve of Marsha! Still fuming, Allison sipped her tea, but then suddenly an awful realization hit her. If Lola came regularly to sort the mail and water the plants, that meant she could pop in unexpected—at any time! She glanced around the apartment. It looked as if Hurricane Allison had hit.

She quickly located the maid's closet and threw herself into fast gear. Sweeping, mopping, scrubbing, and dusting, Allison had never worked so hard in her life. After what felt like hours, the place was at last spotless and looked just the same as when she'd come. The furniture was shrouded, the bedroom and bath straight, and the kitchen shone. Allison wasn't sure what to do with the laundry. For the time being it could occupy the spare room closet since it was empty anyway.

Allison prowled the apartment. Her sense of freedom and fun were now gone. She felt like a caged animal. All thanks to stupid old Lola!

"I've got to escape," she said out loud. "Before I go nuts." Chocolate cream pie sounded delicious. She had spotted a little mom-and-pop cafe on her way back to the apartment yesterday. Maybe she could sit there and think.

Allison searched Marsha's closet, being especially careful not to disturb anything this time. She didn't want to leave any traces of her presence for Lola, and she wasn't eager to hang up any more clothes today. No wonder Marsha had a maid. At last Allison selected a peach rayon suit and matching peach pumps with dainty straps. She clipped on some pearl earrings and patted her chic hairstyle into place. Today she chose a white straw hat, which she perched lightly on her head as she rode the elevator to the lobby. She'd rather go hatless, but Marsha had always said ladies must wear hats and gloves in the city.

Out on the street, a sailor in a crisp white uniform eyed her and whistled his approval. This time Allison smiled but looked straight ahead, keeping her chin up with confidence. She wasn't about to be intimidated.

The pie was just what she needed, and she washed it down with heavily creamed coffee. But she wasn't ready to leave the cozy little cafe yet. A matronly woman poured her another cup of coffee and smiled kindly. Allison looked at the woman and wished she were her grandma.

She knew she was never going to last the summer in New York City. She hated it already. What had she gotten herself into? And what was she going to do about it? She felt reluctant to admit it, but even horrible Camp Wannatonka might have been better than this!

When she felt she'd worn out her welcome at the cafe, Allison stepped out into the late afternoon sunshine. She walked and walked until the pretty peach pumps pinched her toes with every step. It was rush-hour traffic again, and everyone hurried home, eager to escape the city. *Home,* she thought in frustration. *I have no home!* Before Nanny Jane's death, she'd pretend that Nanny Jane's little cottage was her home. It had always made her feel warm and wanted. Now she had nothing . . . no one.

Back at the apartment, she rode the crowded elevator up in silence. Stepping out on the seventeenth floor, she discreetly looked both ways before she let herself into the apartment. Everything looked exactly the same. The mail still lay heaped by the door just as it had fallen. But something on top of the pile caught her eye. It was the name on the return address that stopped her. O'Brian was printed in big, bold letters. That was *her* name!

She picked it up and examined it closely. It was addressed to Marsha and marked personal. The return address showed that it had come all the way from Tamaqua Point, Oregon. Where in the world was that? She knew Oregon was somewhere out west near California. Perhaps it was from someone on her father's side—although she'd been told he had no living relatives. Well, it wouldn't be the first time she'd been deceived.

Should she open it? After all, if it was her relative it might concern her. She ran to the kitchen and put on the teakettle. Carefully steaming the envelope open, she pulled out the letter. The writing was shaky and difficult to read.

June 15, 1948
Dear Marsha,

I know you probably won't answer this letter, as you've never answered any, but this will likely be my final one. The doctor says I may not last the summer, so I'll ask you once again. Yes, I know you've heard it a hundred times. You even went to the trouble to convince me that Allison was dead once. But I know better now. Allison's nanny, Jane McAllister, bless her heart, wrote to me last year. I know Allison is alive!

I wrote to Allison at school many times this past year, but I never heard from her. I'm certain you arranged to have my letters returned. I beg you, Marsha (and I've never begged anyone), if there's a spark of kindness in you, please let me meet my granddaughter before I leave this earthly life. I've enclosed plenty of money to pay for her fare. If she can't come, please give it to her from me—or else burn it!

> *Sincerely and for the last time,*
> *Riley O'Brian*

Allison read the simple words again and again. Her eyes filled with tears for the sadness of this old man. Could it be true? Did she actually have a real, live grandfather? And why hadn't anyone ever told her? She remembered one of Nanny Jane's favorite phrases. *"Darling, things are not always as they seem. . . ."*

Well, it was settled. She was going to Oregon, and wherever this Tamaqua Point was—even if it was at the very end of the earth—she was going there! She would meet this grandfather. To think he had been trying so desperately to get in touch with her, and Marsha had been preventing it!

Her fury at the way Marsha had manipulated her life was instantly replaced with a sense of urgency. She must prepare to leave at once. He'd mentioned money—sure enough, there in the envelope lay a money order in her name for one hundred and fifty dollars! She called the train station and reserved a ticket westbound on the 7:40.

Allison returned to Marsha's closet, where she'd seen several suitcases stacked in the back. Marsha had at least four sets of luggage. Allison hesitated for a moment when she realized she'd be practically stealing her mother's things.

"Am I a thief?" Allison asked out loud. "No, these things are my mother's, and she should be willing to loan them. After all, this is an emergency." Her words didn't completely convince her, but she wondered why she should even care after all that Marsha had done.

She found what appeared to be an older set of suitcases, a large one with two smaller matching bags. They were dark leather trimmed in brass. Probably not Marsha's current style. As Allison pulled them out from the depths of the closet, she noticed a little hidden door with a lock. What could that be? Allison scolded herself. She didn't have time to investigate—she needed to pack.

Allison carefully selected items she thought she might need and what Marsha would never miss. She packed the clothes she'd already worn plus several pairs of trousers, sweaters, blouses, and other pieces she felt might come in handy. Then she threw a raincoat on top and several pairs of shoes. She remembered her flannel nightgown and the bottle of perfume she had bought at Macy's, as well as a few "borrowed" toiletries from Marsha's fathomless supply.

To begin her trip, Allison decided to wear the celery green suit. Although the skirt was difficult to maneuver about in, it definitely made her look older than her fourteen years. She didn't want anyone to suspect she was too young to travel on her own. The green suede pumps, a hat with a gorgeous purple feather, and a handbag completed her ensemble. She twirled before the mirror and the skirt flared out at the hemline. Her heart fluttered with anticipation. She was going to Oregon!

She was about to lock the suitcase when she realized she'd forgotten lingerie. She dug through the tall chest again and found some pieces that would have to do for a while. Maybe she could pick up some more suitable things later. Just as she was about to close the drawer, she again spotted the odd music box. The bittersweet tones of *Swan Lake* filled the air when she opened it—such a hauntingly sad song. She was about to close the lid when the glint of a small brass key caught her eye. Could that possibly fit the secret door? It would drive her crazy if she didn't at least give it a try.

Wedged between stacks of hat boxes and fur coats, she slipped in the key and turned. Magically, the small door popped open. A very large lacquered box was nested inside. Perhaps this was Marsha's good jewelry. It surprised Allison to think Marsha would leave it behind. Everyone knew that Marsha Madison always wore the real stuff wherever she went.

Allison opened the box. To her disappointment it was mostly empty. Just a few old family pieces probably not stylish enough for Marsha's taste. As Allison fingered an old-fashioned brooch, the underside of the box wiggled just slightly. Allison placed the odd bits of jewelry in her lap and pulled up the false bottom. There she found a folded paper underneath.

February 18, 1942
Dear Marsha,

    I wanted you to know I've been doing some thorough research on behalf of James. I can now prove that he is completely innocent. I've already sent copies of proof to the firm. They have cleared his name and agreed to drop the charges. But I knew you'd want to know so you could contact him as soon as possible. I know he's serving overseas right now. It must be difficult for him after being falsely accused and slandered. I hope you will inform him as soon as possible.

> *Best wishes,*
> *Thomas C. Hardwick*

P.S. Saw your movie—you were fantastic. Didn't know you still had it in you, old girl!

Allison put the box back together and returned it to its hiding place. She locked the door and left the closet looking undisturbed, but she tucked the letter deep into a pocket of her suitcase. She had no idea what it meant, but since James was her father she felt she had a right to the letter. Maybe this explained some of the secrecy. Maybe her grandfather could explain the rest.

Allison went over the apartment once more. She wanted no traces of her visit left behind for that snoop Lola to discover. When she was certain that everything was perfect, she quietly slipped out. She wasn't sad to leave. This wasn't her home. She'd only been an unwanted trespasser. At least now she was going to a place where she had been invited. A place where she was more than wanted. Oh, just to think she had a grandfather. And maybe there were other relatives, too!

She struggled to get her bags quickly into the elevator. Downstairs, the doorman rushed to her aid and carried her luggage out the door.

"Have you a cab, miss?"

"Oh no, I completely forgot!"

"Never you mind." He stepped out and flagged one for her. Allison remembered how Stanley had tipped the doorman before, and she did likewise.

"Have a good trip," he smiled as he shut the cab door.

"Grand Central, please," she told the cabby. She was a little early, but she didn't know what else to do. Besides, she'd always enjoyed watching people at train stations. Trying to figure out where they were going, where they'd been. She'd witnessed scenes, especially during the war years, that could still put a

lump in her throat. Husbands and daddies leaving for war, un-
certain if they'd see their loved ones again. But later, she'd seen
happy reunions, as well. Yes, train stations were an interesting
place to spend a couple spare hours.

Allison got her bags checked in, then she strolled down the
terminal. The smell of roast beef from the station restaurant
tantalized her and reminded her stomach of its emptiness. She
got a table with a view and enjoyed a leisurely meal of roast beef,
potatoes and gravy, biscuits, and a piece of apple pie a la mode.
She couldn't remember when she'd eaten so much.

At the next table there sat a father and mother and their
three children. The girl looked to be around Allison's age, only
she was dressed more like a regular fourteen-year-old. Allison's
cheeks burned when she noticed one of the older boys looking
her direction. He probably had no idea that she was only his kid
sister's age. He had to be at least eighteen or nineteen.

The charade of looking older was still fun, but she looked
forward to the day she could turn back into a carefree fourteen-
year-old. The girl at the other table teased and poked her broth-
ers. Then the family bowed their heads, and Allison stared in
wonder. She'd never actually seen such a thing. Just then the
young man glanced up and caught her gaping. He winked and
bowed his head again. She turned away, her cheeks warm, and
vowed never to be caught staring again.

Allison asked for her check and left quickly, not daring to
look back at the happy family. Her heart burned a little with
jealousy. Why wasn't she the daughter in that family? Who had
dealt her such a life and why?

She bought a magazine and sat on a deserted bench in her
terminal section, flipping through the pages until a fiction story
captured her attention. The next thing she knew the conductor
was shouting, "All aboard!"

Allison grabbed her things, found her ticket, and hurried
toward the waiting train. Just ahead of her, the family from the

restaurant gathered. She wanted to slip past unnoticed, but the young man finished his good-byes and approached the train. When he saw her coming, he politely stepped aside.

"After you," he gestured with his hand, his blue eyes sparkling merrily.

Allison blushed, looked away, and stepped aboard. The brakes hissed sharply beneath her and she jumped in fright. She felt a hand steady her from behind. The conductor chuckled at her skittishness and punched her ticket.

Allison glanced over her shoulder as she walked down the aisle of the crowded train car. There he was, following right behind her—Mr. Blue Eyes!

Five

AS FATE WOULD HAVE IT, the only seats available were two right next to each other at the front of the car. Allison took the seat by the window and stared at the soot-covered brick wall of the train depot. She glanced at her watch, then wondered why. She had no timetable to regulate her, no deadlines to meet. She anticipated only quiet days with the rhythmic clickety-clack of the wheels on the track, train stations in small towns, new sights, and unfamiliar faces. She must locate a map to chart her cross-country course and perhaps a notebook for a journal. She felt like a butterfly fresh from the cocoon, ready to spread her wings and flutter away.

She turned from the brick wall and noticed the seat still empty beside her. She'd almost forgotten Mr. Blue Eyes. She glanced around, wondering if he had gone on to another car. Was she relieved or disappointed? She peered down the aisle again, puzzled over where he went.

"Looking for someone?" asked a masculine voice from behind.

She turned abruptly in her seat.

"Is this seat taken?"

"Uh . . . I . . . no. I mean, no, it's not taken." She felt her cheeks burn as she gaped at his incredibly handsome face. He folded his newspaper and sat down. She stared blankly out the window and didn't even notice the brick wall slowly pulling away.

She wasn't entirely sure how to act around young men. Having been in a girls' school all these years, she seldom had the opportunity. Sure, she had listened as older girls told what must

49

have been exaggerated stories, but it was still a foreign world to Allison. Well, maybe it was time to learn, and she had better learn fast if she wanted to keep pretending to be a young woman of eighteen.

Should she use her real name? No, she'd stick with Sheila, but not LaVelle. Sheila Jones. Yes, that was believable and easy to remember. Now she needed to concoct a story. She'd just graduated from high school and was traveling west to care for an ailing spinster aunt. Her destination? Not Oregon, that might leave a trail. How about Washington. Wasn't that close by? Yes, Seattle, Washington. She rehearsed these facts in her mind several times and then relaxed.

"Would you like a stick of gum?" Mr. Blue Eyes offered.

"No, thank you." She remembered Miss Snyder's admonition, *"Ladies don't chew gum in public."* Though the minty smell was tempting.

"Are you traveling far?" he asked.

"Yes, as a matter of fact." Now what should she say? She wasn't sure how much information to disclose to a perfect stranger, no matter how blue his eyes were.

"Excuse me," he sounded apologetic. "I should've introduced myself. My name is John Stewart, and I'm from White Plains, New York. I'm on my way to Ohio to spend the summer working at a Christian youth camp on Lake Erie." He paused as if waiting for her response.

"I'm Sheila Jones. I'm from Connecticut, traveling to Seattle, Washington." There! That should keep him happy for a while.

John carried most of the conversation as he described the youth camp in colorful detail. It sounded nothing like Camp Wannatonka. If she'd had an opportunity to attend a camp like that, she might not be on the run right now. Of course, then she might not ever have had the chance to meet her grandfather, either. She thought of the words in his letter and hoped that she wasn't too late.

"You look a little worried," he remarked. "Is everything okay?"

His discernment caught her off guard. "Well, yes, I suppose. I am awfully worried about my aunt—Aunt Eleanor. I'm going to care for her in Seattle. She's very ill—maybe dying . . ."

His blue eyes softened in sympathy. She felt a stab of guilt and wished she had told him the truth. But it was partly true—she was very concerned for an ailing relative.

In a short time they'd passed through New Jersey and entered Pennsylvania. John read his newspaper, and Allison admired the orderly farms scattered across the fertile green countryside. They passed a dairy farm where even the black-and-white cows looked freshly scrubbed.

"Oh, how quaint! A parade!" Allison exclaimed in surprise. Several old-fashioned horse-drawn carriages drove down the road alongside the railroad tracks. The women and children inside the buggies wore dark-colored, old-fashioned clothing, while the men bore full beards and unique straw hats.

"Actually, those are Amish people. They don't believe in modern technology," John informed her.

"Really? No radios or telephones?"

"Nope. They make everything from scratch. Even their tools are handmade. Pretty resourceful, too." John's knowledge impressed her.

Allison noticed an attractive older gentleman limp down the aisle toward them with a wooden leg. She wondered if he'd lost it in the war. At least he had been luckier than her father—he had made it back.

"I think I'll check out the diner," John said, stretching his tall frame. "Want to join me? I saw some tempting pies earlier when I picked up the paper."

"That sounds nice," Allison replied. "Besides, I'd like to

move around a bit. I don't know if I'll survive all this sitting. I wonder how long it takes to get to Ore—I mean Washington." She glanced quickly at John, but he didn't seem to notice her blunder.

In the dining car, the lights were low and most of the diners were just finishing up. John and Allison picked a small table at the back that was covered with a clean white cloth. They both ordered rhubarb pie, and John did most of the talking. That was fine with Allison; he was easy to listen to. Outside it became dusky and the sky turned peachy-pink. Strips of lavender trickled through silhouettes of black trees outlined on the horizon like construction paper cutouts.

"Isn't it beautiful?" exclaimed Allison. "It seems so long since I've seen a real sunset. In New York City you can barely see the sky."

"New York?" John looked at her with a puzzled expression on his face.

"Well, yes . . . I stayed with my sister for a few days in New York before my trip." She covered her error gracefully this time, though her conscience was starting to nag her. Even though it didn't feel right, lying was becoming a little too easy for her and she didn't like it. She didn't want it to become a habit. She'd heard both Marsha and Grandmother tell many lies. Allison had even asked Grandmother about it once, but Grandmother had become very irate and defensive. *"They're only white lies, Allison,"* she had snapped. But Allison had never liked their lies, and she had never wanted to be like them.

"Sheila?" John repeated the phony name again, looking at her curiously.

"Oh . . . excuse me. I was just daydreaming," Allison said, her cheeks glowing with embarrassment.

John studied her with a puzzled expression, as if he suspected she was not being completely honest with him. "I just wanted to mention that I noticed some travel brochures and maps up there on the counter. If you're interested . . ." They went up and browsed through the rack. While Allison picked out a map and travel log, she noticed that John was paying their bill.

"John, I didn't expect you to pay for my pie," she said indignantly.

"It's not every day I get to take a pretty girl out for dessert." His blue eyes twinkled.

"Thank you. I guess it's getting late. . . ." She wasn't quite sure what to say. She didn't really want to find her sleeping car yet, but she felt foolish just loitering about.

"Would you like another cup of tea?" he offered, looking hopeful. She agreed, and before she knew it they had talked for another hour.

"You know, Sheila, I don't mean to snoop, but you seem a little mysterious to me. Are you running from something?" He looked straight into her eyes this time.

She turned her gaze down to the silver teaspoon in her hand and nervously fingered the train's monogram engraved on the handle. John seemed like such a caring person. Could she trust him with part of her story? It wouldn't hurt to try. . . .

"I'm not exactly running *from* something . . . but I hope maybe *to* something." She drew in a deep breath and went on to tell him about her grandfather.

"Don't you think it would have been better to tell your mother the truth?" he asked sincerely.

"Maybe, but she was unavailable." John lifted a suspicious eyebrow and Allison laughed. "No, really, that one's true. My mother's out of the country right now."

He smiled. "Well, you seem like a nice kid and I was just concerned. I hope you don't think I'm butting in. I guess if you were my little sister, I'd be pretty worried about you traveling across the country alone."

So he saw through my disguise all along, Allison thought.

He'd probably even guessed her age. "How old do you think I am, anyway?" she asked defensively.

"Well, definitely not eighteen. Maybe fifteen or sixteen."

She smiled. She didn't have to tell him everything.

"My point is this, Sheila. Be careful. You're alone, but you don't have to advertise it. You should pair up with trustworthy travelers. Preferably women. But don't trust everyone. And for goodness' sake, don't let strange men buy you pie and tea!"

She nodded, trying to take in all his advice. "You didn't seem strange to me. Besides, I saw you bow your head with your family in the railroad station, remember?" Allison grinned.

"Looks can be deceiving."

Allison remembered Nanny Jane used to say the same thing.

"But this time you were lucky because they weren't." John smiled and pulled out a pad and pen to write down an address. "Let me know how you get along, okay? I'll see you safely to your sleeper." He handed her the slip of paper, and they quickly found her compartment.

"I get off in Cleveland at 5:15 A.M., so this is good-bye, Sheila."

"The name's Allison."

"Much more suitable. Good luck—and remember what I said." He tipped his hat and left.

After she settled herself into her compartment and finished her magazine article, Allison thought about the day's events. She replayed all that John had said that evening, and she felt sorry to see him depart so soon. But she'd take his advice. Her whirling thoughts began to subside, and the repetitive sound of the wheels on the track plus the gentle swaying motion of the train lulled her to sleep.

⚬ ⚬ ⚬

The next morning she bolted awake and clung to the wooden sides of her bunk. Was it an earthquake? *Oh yes, the train,* she reminded herself. "I wonder where we are?" She pulled out her map and tried to estimate. It was 8:15, so it was possible they might still be in Ohio.

She hurriedly dressed and made her way to the diner. In front of her stood the man with the wooden leg. She wondered about his destination. Did he have a family waiting? Maybe he'd just been released from prison camp. She'd heard stories about prisoners of war only recently freed. She shuddered to imagine the horrors of Nazi prison camps.

Just behind her waited a lone woman. Allison remembered John's words and discreetly tried to examine the lady. She wore a fine wool traveling suit the color of bleached driftwood. Her silver hair was coiled in a loose bun, and she carried a book under her arm. Allison tilted her head slightly to read the title.

"Do you like poetry, dear?" asked the woman with a smile.

"Oh yes," Allison answered honestly, but her face reddened when she recognized her sleuthing skills needed polish. The lady showed Allison her book, *Great American Poets.*

"I couldn't help but notice your interest. Are you eating alone?" The woman glanced around. "Maybe you'd like to join me?"

"Yes, I'd love to."

At last they were seated in the busy dining car. Allison ordered ham and eggs and orange juice.

"My name is Amanda Pierce," the lady said, carefully unfolding her napkin. "I'm a retired English professor, and I'm traveling to Des Moines to visit my daughter. I haven't seen her for three years and she has a new baby girl. They named her Amanda Constance after me. I can't wait to hold her!"

Allison smiled. This woman seemed safe enough.

After breakfast they visited some more and watched the wheat and cornfields whiz by. Amanda, as she insisted Allison call her, loaned her an Emily Dickinson book. They read peacefully and took short breaks to discuss their reading.

Amanda retired for a nap in the afternoon, and Allison returned to her sleeping car. Inspired by Emily Dickinson, she picked up her pen and attempted a poem. She'd written other short poems in school and found poetry fun, but this poem actually expressed something from deep within her.

"The Long Way Home"
by Allison O'Brian.

I travel a secluded path that I must walk alone.
What lies around the next bend to me remains unknown.
I see the others passing by, loved ones hand in hand.
It seems they found a shortcut I cannot understand.
The miles, they stretch before me like an endless field of
*   wheat.*
Step by step, I am unsure, I fear I may retreat.
Perhaps I'll reach that other shore, that swirls with milk-
*   white foam,*
Then I'll rejoice in family ties, though I took the long way
*   home.*

She met Amanda for dinner and told her about it. "It's really nothing. Not very good, I'm sure. It just seemed to roll off the top of my head."

"Oh, I'd love to hear it, dear. Maybe I could even give you a pointer or two."

Allison couldn't resist. Amanda sipped her tea while Allison slowly read the poem aloud.

"I know it's not much," began Allison after a long pause, then she noticed Amanda had tears in her eyes.

"No, you're wrong, dear. It was beautiful." Amanda looked at Allison. "You've communicated a message, and that's what poetry is all about."

They discussed poetry all through dinner. Allison was fascinated by Emily Dickinson and her sorrowful life. Amanda seemed to really understand poor Emily, and they talked on into the night.

"As much as I hate to, I must turn in. The train arrives in Des Moines very early. Good night, my dear." Amanda gave Allison a warm hug. "I hope you find your way home."

❧   ❧   ❧

The next morning Allison awoke to stillness. *Must be a stop*, she thought. But it seemed to go on forever. *What's wrong?* she wondered. *Why aren't we moving?* She dressed quickly and hurried out to investigate.

Other curious passengers crowded the aisle in various stages of dress. She made her way to the dining car and looked out the plate-glass window. Blinking her eyes in unbelief, she spied a tiger prowling outside, and beyond him limped a tall giraffe. A couple of chimps clung to the switch signal next to the tracks. Had she gone to sleep and awakened in Africa? A dining car attendant saw her face and laughed.

"Don't be alarmed, miss. A circus train derailed just outside of Omaha. It's taking them a while to clear the tracks . . . not to mention capture the critters. We're going to back up into Omaha for a few hours until it's cleared up."

"Oh my goodness! Was anyone hurt?" Allison looked at the poor giraffe.

"Not that I heard."

They backed into Omaha around nine A.M. Everyone poured from the train in a festive mood, talking about elephants, tigers, and bears. It was like being on safari.

Allison strolled down the main street, surprised to see tall buildings. She'd expected Omaha to be like the western movies, with false-front stores and hitching posts, though she did spy a couple of cowboys.

An old-fashioned drugstore caught her eye, and she stopped for a soda. Red-and-white-striped wallpaper adorned the walls, and the ice-cream counter was constructed of an immense piece of intricately carved oak. Behind it hung an expansive mirror framed by shelves filled with fancy soda glasses and sundae dishes, their images doubled by the sparkling reflection in the mirror. Allison could just imagine a Gibson girl sipping a soda at the turn of the century.

Just as she finished the last delectable drop of her malt, she noticed the man with the wooden leg bolt out the door. *How odd*, she mused as she reached for her purse on the next stool. It wasn't there. She checked the floor. It was gone! Her money, her train ticket, even her grandfather's address! The image of the man with the wooden leg flashed through her memory again and she tore off after him.

"Miss!" called the skinny teen behind the counter. "You forgot to pay for your—"

She flew out the door and looked both ways down the street. Nowhere in sight! How did he get away so fast?

Allison rushed to the train station and searched the area. Police . . . she needed the police. But what if they asked questions? The word *runaway* streaked through her mind. If they realized she was alone, she'd be in trouble for sure. She glanced at her watch. The train was due to leave in ten minutes. She rushed back toward the drugstore. There in front of the ice-cream counter stood a stout policeman jotting down notes.

"Yep, I'd say she was about nineteen or twenty," the teen was saying. "Reddish hair, real purty." She ducked out of sight and slipped down the street. Flattering description, but now they'd be looking for her. What in the world was she to do? She hurried back to the train station. Maybe she could sneak onto the train.

The conductors posted by each entrance greeted passengers and joked about the circus roundup. But they also diligently checked passage tickets. She watched for her chance in silent desperation. Her heart pounded with fear, and tears filled her eyes. How could this happen? *Oh, God, help me*, she cried in her heart and buried her face in her hands.

"All aboard!" crooned the conductor one last time.

Six

"HOLD ON, THERE!" shouted a voice from the other end of the terminal. "Hold the train!"

Allison looked up. The man with the wooden leg was waving his hand and yelling. She leaped up in rage. "You! You!" She pointed her finger at him, her face still wet from tears as he limped toward her. He was hauling a scruffy-looking youth behind him. The conductor whistled to the engineer and signaled him to wait.

"Are you Allison O'Brian?" the man gasped, rubbing his leg above the wooden peg. His face grimaced in pain.

"Yes," she answered honestly. She was finally finished with Sheila Jones.

"I believe this is yours," he said as he handed her purse to her. "Make sure everything's there." He turned to the conductor. "This crook stole the young lady's purse back in town. I chased him down, but I don't know what to do with him now." The fellow scowled and tried to wrench from his grip, but the man held tight. "I don't want to miss my train." A small group of bystanders had gathered around them.

"Here, we'll take the scoundrel off your hands," said a burly-looking cowboy. He took the teen by the collar. "We'll be right happy to hand him over to the police."

The conductor escorted Allison and the man with the wooden leg onto the train, and the crowd clapped and cheered as the train pulled away.

"How can I thank you?" Allison asked. She quickly looked inside her purse. "Everything seems to be here." Tears slipped down her cheeks again, but this time they were from relief.

"Well, for one thing, I'm starved. I had to leave behind a nice hot fudge sundae to catch your thief. Maybe you could take me to lunch." He brushed the dust off his jacket.

"Of course . . ." She didn't know what else to say.

He grinned. "When I saw that fella grab your bag and head for the door, I remembered you from the train—you remind me of my own daughter."

She smiled. "Well, I can't thank you enough. Now you must let me get you some lunch, Mr.—"

"James O'—"

"Excuse me," interrupted a heavyset woman as she squeezed past them and on down the aisle. Allison's mouth dropped open and she stared at the man, waiting for him to repeat his name. Could it possibly be?

"Are you all right, Allison?" he asked with concern. "You look like you've seen a ghost."

"Your name . . . what's your name?"

"James O'Conner." He looked at her curiously.

She shook her head. "I'm sorry. I don't know what came over me. I thought you were going to say that you were James O'Brian. I know it's silly, but that was my dad's name. He was killed in the war. I never really knew him. . . ."

"Oh, I see." He nodded as if he understood. "Well, you've had quite a shock today. We probably both need to sit down and regain our wits." He guided her to the dining car. They were quickly seated at a table. Mr. O'Conner ordered a cup of coffee, and she ordered tea. She sipped it silently, thinking how foolish she was to have, even for a moment, supposed this man could have been her father. How ridiculous!

"You know . . . I remember meeting a James O'Brian in England during the war."

"Really? In England? Do you think it could have been my dad?" Allison looked at him hopefully.

He frowned. "No, I guess not. This James O'Brian was in

the hospital. It was the same time I was there for my leg. But he was getting shipped back home. And you say your dad was killed in the war. . . ." He shook his head sadly. "I'm sorry."

"I suppose that would be impossible," Allison said quietly. "I'm sure there could have been many men with the same names." Allison tried to smile. "I guess it's silly for me to even think it . . . but sometimes I get this odd feeling that he could be alive. It's stupid of me. . . ."

"No, it's not stupid, Allison. Death is odd like that. I know during the war—" He looked out the window for a long moment. "Sometimes we'd lose someone, but it just wouldn't seem real. You'd expect to see him walk up any time. Finally I came to the point where I just had to trust God and believe in heaven—that hopefully he'd just gone on to heaven ahead of me. Like your dad, Allison."

She set her cup down. "Maybe so. I don't really understand death or heaven very well."

"I don't know anyone who actually understands it with their head. It's more in your heart." Mr. O'Conner rubbed his chin and studied her. "You're looking a little better now. For a moment back there I thought you were going to faint. Take a glance out the window. Can you believe that incredible landscape? It's just like something out of a western movie."

Allison gazed out the window. It did look like true cowboy country with lonely prairie, mesa rocks, and a scraggly herd of steer grazing off in the distance.

"What was your father like, Allison?"

"Well . . ." How could she say this without sounding like a complete idiot? "Actually, I don't really know. I can't even remember what he looked like. I'm not even sure if I ever saw him. But"—she tapped her chest—"down here I feel like I knew him. And, of course, my nanny used to tell me good things about him. He was an artist."

He smiled. "I'm sure you did know him in your heart, and

I'm confident he was a fine man. Maybe someday you can learn more about him."

"Yes, and that's exactly what I'm intending to do."

Mr. O'Conner looked up. "And how's that?"

She was tired of all the lies about her trip. The shock in Omaha broke something in her, and she was determined to play things as straight as possible from here on out. Besides, something made her trust Mr. O'Conner. She told him all about her strange trip and how she hoped to meet her grandfather.

"Oregon!" he exclaimed. "Well, that's just where I'm bound. I'm on my way back from Europe. I swore I would never go back to that awful place after the war, but we heard about a clinic over there that designs artificial limbs for people. It's called a prosthesis, and they're almost like the real thing. They have joints and everything. But in order to have my leg fitted properly, I had to go in person. My uncle Henry has more money than you can shake a stick at, and he insisted on funding all my travel expenses and everything. My family just wouldn't let me say no."

"Oh, Mr. O'Conner, that's wonderful! So did you get one— a pro-whatever—a leg, I mean?" Allison asked.

He chuckled. "Yes, I did. But it wasn't completely finished when I left. They'll ship it to me soon. I was just too eager to get back to my family. Besides, it's still a mess over there, and so many bad memories . . ."

Allison tried to imagine. It must have been horrible. "You mentioned a daughter."

"Yes, my Sharon. She just turned thirteen. That's thirteen going on twenty-three. And I have a sixteen-year-old son, Mark, who's just learned to drive, heaven help us. He also works part time as a box boy at the supermarket."

Allison sensed the deep love this father had for his children. She felt happy for them in a bittersweet sort of way. She wondered if they realized how fortunate they were.

She spent the rest of the afternoon reading more from *The Life and Times of Emily Dickinson*. Amanda had inscribed the book and given it to Allison. She read the words again. *To Allison, Life's struggles can often lead us to ourselves. Don't lose heart on the winding road for home. Love, Amanda.* Allison closed the cover and for the first time noticed the author's name: A.C. Pierce. Wasn't Amanda's last name Pierce? And hadn't she said her granddaughter, Amanda Constance, was named after her? Could it be the Amanda she'd met was actually A.C. Pierce? Allison remembered Amanda's praise and promised herself to faithfully continue to write poetry, even if no one ever read another word of it.

ဆ ဆ ဆ

She joined Mr. O'Conner for dinner. The vast prairie stretched out before them as far as the eye could see.

"It's amazing," Allison remarked. "Nebraska just seems to go on and on. We've traveled for hours and the landscape hardly changes."

"Can you imagine how the pioneers must have felt? They traveled at only a fraction of our speed."

"Well, I'll say this for Nebraska," said Allison between bites. "They do have good steaks."

He laughed. "Allison, with you around my trip should go a little faster. I hate being away from my family. I thought after the war I'd never have to leave them again. My Susan, she's a real trooper. She managed to keep those kids in line while I was gone and hold down a job, too. Now she's talking about going back to work, though I'm not too sure about that. I always thought a woman's place was in the home. Say, you've never mentioned your mother. Did she marry again?"

Allison groaned. Here was a subject she detested. "Let me put it this way. She's not exactly the domestic type. And yes, she married again—twice!"

Mr. O'Conner's eyes opened wide.

"Well, not twice at once. I mean, first she married this movie producer—" *Oops*, she thought. *I said too much.* Now he looked extremely curious. "Can you keep a secret, Mr. O'Conner?" she spoke confidentially. "Do you know who Marsha Madison is?"

"Sure, everyone knows who Marsha Ma—" He looked at her in amazement. "No, you're kidding?"

She nodded and smiled.

"You're kidding!" he said again.

Allison got a kick out of his reaction. "Yep, that's my mom, believe it or not. And just for the record, I am not very proud of her. I'm sorry to say that a lot of the nasty stuff they write about her is true."

He whistled, shaking his head. "Why, I never would've guessed in a thousand years."

&ca; &ca; &ca;

The next morning they were out of Nebraska and passing through Wyoming, but the scenery remained much the same. Allison played cards with Mr. O'Conner in the afternoon. An elderly woman commented on how nice it was to see father and daughter traveling together so congenially. Mr. O'Conner didn't correct her and Allison felt flattered. If she could choose a father, he would be just like Mr. O'Conner.

Later in the afternoon the landscape changed. They were in the foothills of the Rockies now, rough and rugged country. Mr. O'Conner was great at spotting wildlife. They saw a big horned sheep, a few coyote, elk, and lots of antelope. Mr. O'Conner even tried to photograph them from the train.

&ca; &ca; &ca;

The train passed through the mountains that night, and Allison awoke to a peculiar light. She stood up on her bunk and rubbed the condensation off the tiny window of her sleeper. The full moon was shining brightly in the crystal clear sky, and the snow-covered rocks reflected it with a bluish glow. It looked unreal, like another world or perhaps the surface of the moon. She watched for a long time, feeling insignificant and small out in the middle of nowhere. She pressed her cheek against the cold glass and listened to the rhythm of the steel wheels as they traveled down the tracks, feeling very much alone. Would it always be like this?

She wondered about her grandfather. Was it too late? Would he still be alive? Would he be glad to see her?

∞   ∞   ∞

The next day they crossed the border into Oregon. Allison and Mr. O'Conner threw a private party at lunch to celebrate.

"Here's to Oregon." Mr. O'Conner toasted his root beer high.

"Here's to a good homecoming!" agreed Allison with her cola.

Later on, she looked out over the massive Columbia River in awe. The mountains of the gorge seemed to jut right out of the water. Then they passed the majestic Multnomah Falls, and Mr. O'Conner described its beautiful scenery. Allison hoped maybe someday she could return to see the falls. Mr. O'Conner pointed out Mount Hood and told her all about the skiing there.

"Well, Allison, we'll be in Portland soon. Do you have your connections made to get you to your grandfather's?"

"I hadn't really thought that far ahead. I just figured I'd catch the next train. I don't think Tamaqua Point is too far from Portland."

Mr. O'Conner laughed. "It might not be that simple. Unfortunately, there are no trains that go to the coast. I'm not even sure about buses. Do you have a place to stay in Portland if you're laid over?"

Allison looked at her hands and frowned. She hadn't

stopped to consider how she'd get to the coast from Portland. When she'd looked at her map, Portland seemed so close to her final destination.

"Well, you're welcome to stay with me and my family," Mr. O'Conner smiled warmly at her. "And we'll help you figure out a way to get you safely to your grandfather."

Allison beamed. "Oh, thank you so much. That's such a relief."

"We're not exactly the Ritz, but we know how to be hospitable."

Allison stuck with Mr. O'Conner for the rest of the trip and at the train station. He helped her round up her bags, then they made their way to the terminal where his whole family awaited him. She instantly recognized them from earlier conversations. The petite blond woman with a sweet face would be Mrs. O'Conner, and the girl with the mischievous twinkle in her eye would be Sharon. Of course the tall young man who definitely took after his father was Mark. Allison stood back shyly as Mr. O'Conner greeted and hugged his family. It was one of those perfect train station reunions she loved to watch.

"Allison, I'm Susan, and this is Sharon and Mark," Mr. O'Conner's wife said. "And we'd love to have you spend the night with us!" The boy smiled and took her bags.

"You can stay in my room!" Sharon said with enthusiasm. "I just adore your outfit. My dad says you're from New York. That must be so exciting. I want to go to New York someday—or maybe Hollywood." She paused to blow a bubble with her gum, then snapped it noisily. "That's where all the action is—Hollywood, you know. You see, I plan to be an actress someday."

Allison gasped silently as they walked across the wet pavement. But Sharon didn't miss a beat. She talked nonstop all the way to the car.

"I'll drive us home, Dad," Mark proclaimed proudly.

"Heaven help us!" cried Mr. O'Conner in mock fear.

Actually, Mark drove very carefully, almost too carefully. Allison wondered if they'd ever get there. She admired the many tall evergreens as they made their way up a winding road. Everything seemed very green and very wet.

The O'Conner home, they informed Allison, had been built after the war. It was a sweet little house with dormer windows tucked into the roof. Mrs. O'Conner had a feast prepared. Baked ham and potatoes, homemade biscuits, coleslaw, and fruit salad.

"Well, this sure beats train food, eh, Allison?" Mr. O'Conner quipped.

"You said it. This is fabulous, Mrs. O'Conner. I can't remember the last time I even had a home-cooked meal." And that was the truth.

Later Allison joined Mark and Sharon in the family room for a game of Monopoly. Before long, Allison was winning.

"Where does your grandfather live?" Mark asked as he landed on Allison's Boardwalk.

"Don't you try to distract me! You owe me some money. Now, pay up. And he lives in a place called Tamaqua Point. Sounds like an Indian name."

"Here's your money. You should've warned us you were the Wolf of Wall Street," Mark teased. "And just for that I won't offer to drive you, because I was considering it and I even happen to know where Tamaqua Point is."

Sharon laughed. "I don't know if you should be relieved or insulted, Allison. At the rate Mark drives, you probably wouldn't make it to Tamaqua Point for at least three days!"

"True. I could probably walk there faster." Allison smirked.

"That's right, go ahead and gang up against me. I'm tough, I can take it."

"Then fork it over, big brother. Because you landed on my Vermont and I just put up a hotel," Sharon announced. Mark rolled to the floor as if mortally wounded while the girls giggled.

"Hate to break up the party, but it's getting a little late. We need to decide how to get Allison to her grandfather's."

"I would have gladly driven her if she hadn't robbed me," Mark exclaimed. Mr. O'Conner looked puzzled, then noticed the game. "Honestly, Dad. I could drive her if it's okay. I've been doing really great. Just ask Mom. And I know how to get to Tamaqua Point easily. Tomorrow's Sunday, so I don't work, and I don't suppose it would kill me to miss church."

"Hmm, but how does Allison feel about this? Is she willing to put her life in your hands?"

"Dad!" Mark exclaimed.

"It might work, but let me talk to your mother first. You know she runs this household now. She just keeps me around for my good looks." He winked at Allison.

Soon it was settled. Mark would drive Allison and they would leave right after breakfast. Knowing what the next day held in store for her, Allison wanted to go to sleep as soon as possible. She followed Sharon to her room.

Allison liked Sharon's little room. There were twin beds with matching lavender coverlets, just the color of spring violets, and priscilla curtains framed the window.

"Sharon, your room is so sweet and cozy," Allison complimented as she sat on the bed.

"Oh, thanks. My mom sewed the curtains and stuff, but I picked it all out. Lavender is my favorite color, you know," she said proudly.

Allison didn't mind Sharon's incessant chatter as they prepared for bed. Sharon continued talking even after the lights were turned off. But it didn't matter since Allison could hardly sleep anyway. Tomorrow she'd meet her grandfather for the very first time—if only his health had held out. It'd been almost two weeks since he'd written, but to Allison it seemed a lifetime. What if something had happened to him? Perhaps she should have telegrammed him of her arrival.

"Allison, are you asleep?" Sharon whispered.

"No, I was just thinking. . . ."

"Well, I was just curious if you ever go to the theater in New York. You know . . . the Broadway productions?"

"Oh sure. I went to one just last Christmas." Allison remembered going with Marsha and Stanley. She'd felt so out of place. Everyone was in jewels and furs, and she'd looked like a little schoolgirl in the red woolen coat that Lola had bought for her with Marsha's money.

"Broadway. . . ." Sharon sighed dreamily. "I think that would be so exciting. I think I'll go to New York and aim for the theater. It's probably more exhilarating than motion pictures," Sharon stated dramatically. "Besides, I hear it's easier to get started in theater and then move on to films afterward."

"Sharon," Allison said with real concern. "Do you really think you'd like it? From all I've heard it can be a horribly demanding life." Allison wouldn't wish the life of an actress on anyone, and especially not dear Mr. O'Conner's daughter.

"Oh no, I think it'd be thrilling and glamorous! You get to wear beautiful clothes, meet other famous people, and go to all of the best parties."

"I suppose so. . . . But there's another side, too. An actress loses a lot. She can lose her family and even her privacy. And it seems with every production she loses her individuality. Some even lose their morals."

"Oh, Allison, you make it sound just awful. What makes you such an expert, anyway? Just because you live in New York doesn't mean you know everything. I know a lot about actresses. I even read movie magazines."

Sharon sounded irritated and Allison wondered if she should just let it go, but somehow she thought Mr. O'Conner might appreciate it if she could give Sharon some good advice.

"Sharon, I suppose you've heard of Marsha Madison."

"Of course! I just saw her in *Desert Rose*. She's an amazing actress. I just love her movies. I heard she started out on Broadway."

"She's my mother."

"Oh sure, and I'm Elizabeth Taylor! Come on, Allison, I wasn't born yesterday."

"Well, she is. And I can attest to the fact that her life is nothing to strive for. At least I know I wouldn't want it."

"You're making this up, Allison. I bet my dad put you up to this just to discourage me."

"No, Sharon. In fact, I don't usually tell people about my mother. Frankly, she embarrasses me. She's never been a mother to me. She practically gave me to my grandmother as a baby, and she makes me call her Marsha and pretend I'm her sister. I've spent the last eight years in boarding school, and I would give anything, *anything*, to have what you have! And you just take it for granted."

"What do you mean?"

"You don't realize how lucky you are to have a home and a family that loves you. I've seen firsthand how the life of an actress can destroy all those things." Sharon was silent. Allison wondered if she'd said too much.

"Do you mean it? Is Marsha Madison really your mother?"

"Yes, and if you don't believe me I can prove it." Allison still had the letter from her grandfather addressed to Marsha.

"No, Allison. I believe you. I'm just in shock! It's so incredible. . . . Marsha Madison's daughter right here in my bedroom!"

Allison laughed. "Well, I didn't mean to rain on your parade, but I thought you should know what it's really like."

Sharon thanked her and chattered on and on about how amazing it was to know someone famous. Allison only hoped that somehow her words of advice would be remembered somewhere down the line. At least she had tried.

"How can I ever repay you for your hospitality?" Allison asked the next day as she said her good-byes to the O'Conners.

"You just take care and enjoy your visit with your grandfather," Mr. O'Conner answered kindly.

Allison and Mark loaded the car up with her bags. She took a moment to thank the O'Conners one more time for opening their home up to her. She didn't know what she would have done without them. Then she was on her way.

Mark carefully navigated the bulky Packard over the maze of bridges and out of town. Allison didn't mind his cautiousness so much now and felt she was in good hands.

"Allison, Sharon told me about your mother. I could hardly believe it. But then, there is something about you . . . I mean, I can imagine you being the daughter of a celebrity." Mark said it in such a flattering way it made her blush.

She admired the rugged terrain as they traveled through the coastal mountains. Nothing like the Rockies, but still a bit untamed in a milder way. They passed some heavily loaded logging trucks climbing slowly up the hills.

"Do you realize that just one of those logs could probably build a couple of homes?" Mark told her informatively.

She couldn't begin to imagine. Actually, all she could think about was her grandfather. What would he be like? Would he be ailing in bed, barely holding on to life? What if she was too late? She couldn't think about that. What would he think of her? What if he didn't like her? Would there be a grandmother or any other relatives?

"You can see the ocean when we come over this hill," Mark informed her, breaking into her thoughts.

Her heart beat a little faster. There on the horizon lay a thin strip of blue. "That's it! I can see it! It's the first time I've seen the Pacific Ocean. Marsha promised once to take me to the West Coast and Hollywood, but it never happened. I don't care, though. I'd rather see it like this." Allison smiled.

They drove down the twisting highway along the cliffs over-looking the coastline. Mark was painstakingly cautious. She knew it was for the best, but just the same, she wished he'd step on it. Allison distracted herself with the fascinating land-scape. It wasn't at all like the East Coast. Though she couldn't put her finger on it, for some reason she liked it better. A fog bank rolled in off the ocean. Soon they were draped in it, like a giant gray blanket, thick and dense.

"We're almost there. Maybe I should stop at a service station to find out exactly where your grandfather's place is," Mark suggested. They entered the tiny town of Tamaqua Point, population 987, and found a small gas station.

"O'Brians'? Yep, it's just round the next bend." The uni-formed attendant looked into the car curiously. "You'll see the lighthouse, then about a mile, I'd guess."

The lighthouse was shrouded in fog, but they could make out the light flashing steadily. Allison held her breath around the bend—she couldn't believe this was happening. She spotted a white mailbox on the edge of the highway with *O'Brian* sten-ciled in big black letters.

"That's it," she almost screamed. Mark pulled off onto the shoulder next to the gravel driveway and started to drive in.

"No, Mark. Don't pull in. I know it's silly, but I want to walk in alone. We can just set my bags by that tree. I'll get them later."

"But what if no one's here? What if they're not expecting you? I can't just dump you on the side of the road." Mark looked at her with serious eyes.

"Mark, really, thank you so much for bringing me, but this is something I must do alone. If it doesn't work . . . well . . . I'll figure something out. Who knows, I may be back at your house by tomorrow," she said, trying to sound light and cheerful.

"Okay, Allison. You just take care. You've got our phone number, so call if you need anything, understand?"

She nodded, then threw open the car door and scrambled out.

She waited until the taillights of the Packard pulled out of the driveway, but she noticed the brake lights flash and saw the car park on the side of the road. *That Mark*, she groaned inwardly.

Allison walked down the long gravel drive with no idea of what to expect. Maybe a cozy cottage like Nanny Jane's. Or maybe a tumbledown old shack. She had once heard that her father came from poor people, but then, she'd heard a lot of mistaken information about her family.

The lonely sound of a foghorn sent chills down her spine. Was that a house ahead? She distinguished a large, darkened silhouette in the fog. It looked neither warm nor friendly.

Allison's heart began to pound. What if this was a big mistake? What if her grandfather was a terrible ogre? Or worse yet, what if she was already too late?

 Seven

THE CLOSER ALLISON DREW to the house, the bigger it became. Through the fog she discerned what looked like a Victorian shape, two or three stories high, with some kind of turret or tower on top. The windows were dark. What if, like Mark said, no one was home? Of course, with her grandfather so ill, he might be resting in bed. The house created an eerie image in the swirling mist. She almost yearned to turn back. Almost. Bravely, she walked on.

"Hey there!" yelled a man's voice. "What are you doing?"

Allison jumped in fright, then noticed a large man digging near the house. He wore tall rubber boots and work clothes. He was probably the gardener.

"Hello. I'm looking for a Mr. O'Brian. A Mr. Riley O'Brian." She attempted to calm her quavering voice.

The man, apparently planting a tree, made no move in her direction and continued to dig. "What do you want with him?" he asked suspiciously as he leaned upon his shovel.

How rude, Allison thought. Then she remembered another one of Nanny Jane's sayings. "You catch more flies with honey than vinegar." Perhaps if she turned on her charm he would tell her something about her grandfather. "I've come to inquire on Mr. O'Brian's health. How is he doing?" she asked politely.

"Who wants to know?"

"I do. Is he all right? I know he's been very ill."

"What are you, some sort of nurse?"

"No. Actually, I'm a relative."

"Humph," he grunted. "Probably came to leech off the poor old geezer—maybe get yourself into his will?"

"I most certainly did not!" She'd had enough of his insolence and headed for the front door.

The man dashed over and cut her off on the big covered porch. "Just a minute, missy!" He blocked her way with his bulky frame. "Who should we say is calling?"

"Miss Allison O'Brian," she stated indignantly, tired of the cat-and-mouse game.

The shovel fell from his hands and he clutched his chest. "Allison," he gasped. "You've come!"

"Grandfather?" She helped him through the front door and eased him to a nearby chair. His face was turning gray as it contorted with pain. He reached into his shirt pocket and quickly slipped a couple of tiny pills into his mouth.

"Oh, Grandfather, I'm so sorry I shocked you like that. I didn't know it was you. Please don't die," she sobbed, clenching his rough tweed jacket.

An elderly woman rushed down the hall. She grabbed a blanket from a closet and put it over him. "Now, calm down, Mr. O'Brian. Breathe slowly." She grabbed the phone and called the doctor.

"Help me get him to the den," the woman commanded. They struggled to haul him into the den and settled him on the couch, pulling the blanket over him. Gradually the color returned to his face.

"Now, now, you two take it easy," he said slowly. "It's just another one of my spells, Muriel. You didn't go call Dr. Hartley, now, did you?"

"I sure did, Mr. O'Brian, and he'll be here before too long."

Grandfather groaned. "I don't need that old horse doctor looking at me. I'm going to be fine. I feel better already. All I need is a good cup of tea."

"Humph! What you need is a good spanking. Dr. Hartley told you not to do any hard work, but do you listen? Out there digging like a madman, planting trees—just begging for another heart attack!"

"The trees had nothing to do with it—"

"Yes, I'm so terribly sorry," Allison interrupted. "I'm sure it's all my fault. I didn't mean to startle you so. I . . . I thought you were the gardener. I mean, you didn't look like you could be my . . . my grandfather." She smiled and reached for his hand.

"Grandfather?" Muriel exclaimed. Now it was her turn to be astonished. "Is this—can it be? Little Allison all grown up?"

Allison nodded solemnly.

"Well, take off your hat and coat, dear. I'll turn on the lights and we'll have a look at you." Muriel scurried about turning on lights. Allison removed her hat, and Grandfather and Muriel stared in amazement.

"Mercury," he breathed. Muriel nodded, mouth gaping wide.

Allison shook her head quizzically. "What do you mean? That's my middle name."

Grandfather gestured to the portrait above the fireplace. Muriel flipped a switch and the picture glowed to life. There, poised in an emerald gown, was a lovely young woman. Her skin was like ivory, and her hair was a deep, rich auburn that glowed like firelight. Allison sensed a vague familiarity in the face.

"Mercury Victoria Patterson O'Brian . . . your grandmother. God rest her soul," he spoke the words lovingly, and a bit of Irish brogue slipped off his tongue.

Allison drew near the painting. "She's beautiful, Grandfather." Suddenly, Allison decided she liked her middle name.

"That she was, lassie. And how she'd have loved to see her bonnie granddaughter."

"Hello," called a friendly yet urgent voice from the hall. "I let myself in. Where's the patient?"

In the blink of an eye, Dr. Hartley swept into the room, placed a stethoscope to Riley O'Brian's chest, and poked a thermometer in his mouth. He rolled up a plaid woolen shirt sleeve and pulled out a blood pressure kit. Allison clung to the back of the leather chair and watched in fear, her knees still wobbling.

"Come with me, my darling," Muriel said. She wrapped her arm around Allison's shoulders and led her to the kitchen. "Your grandfather hates doctors. We best leave him be for now."

Muriel dabbed her eyes, straightened her apron, and busied herself at the big black kitchen stove. "I know most people think these woodburning stoves are antiquated, but I still say nothing bakes bread like them. Mr. O'Brian has offered me a fancy electric range dozens of times." She threw some kindling on the smoldering embers and placed a big copper kettle on top.

"Will he be okay?" Allison asked. "Do you think it's serious?"

"I hope not, darling, but we never know. Doc Hartley keeps warning him to take it easy. His heart's still weak from last spring. He was in the hospital for two weeks, you know. I didn't think he was going to make it, but he has a very strong will. And now that *you're* here, I'm sure he'll want to follow the doctor's advice to a tee."

"Oh, I hope you're right. Now that I finally have a grandfather, I couldn't bear to lose him."

Muriel stepped back and took a long, hard look at Allison. "If I remember right, you're only fourteen, but you sure look older."

"I wanted to seem more grown-up—for traveling. So I borrowed some of my mother's clothes. . . ." Allison looked down at her green suede pumps.

"Hmm. And Marsha just let you come, did she?" Muriel asked suspiciously.

Allison could tell that Muriel wasn't one to be fooled. "Well, not exactly. . . ."

"Just as I thought." Muriel prepared a tea tray. "You can fill me in on the details later, but let's not upset your grandfather about it just yet."

Allison nodded. "Can I help you with that, Muriel?"

"Of course not! Guests don't help the staff." Allison jumped back, and Muriel softened and smiled. "Well, all right, dear. Why don't you carry that plate of cookies for me."

Grandfather was sitting up on the couch, bright-eyed and perky, as Dr. Hartley packed the medical equipment back into his worn black doctor bag.

"I think it was just a bit of angina," the doctor announced. "But just the same, I want him to take it easy." This was directed to Muriel.

"Well, now I have an ally. Maybe between the two of us, we may talk some sense into this man." Muriel winked at Allison.

"I certainly hope so. Here's some medicine to help him rest and a prescription for some more digitalis." He handed them to Muriel.

"I hope you'll have some tea," Muriel offered.

"Not this time. Josh Taylor has a mare with a breech foal, and he asked me to stop by. But don't mind if I take a couple of these tasty cookies along."

"See, Allison, what did I tell you? I get sick and they send in the horse doctor," Grandfather complained with a sparkle in his eye.

Dr. Hartley laughed. "Practicing medicine in a small town is a challenge, to say the least." He stepped over to Allison and clasped her hand warmly. "Riley told me about you, Allison. I think it's awfully nice of you to come all the way out here to spend time with him. Now, I better be off before Josh comes hunting me down. Take care—and call if you need me." He patted Grandfather's shoulder and left.

Muriel stirred some life into the dying fire and threw in a couple of small logs. She tucked the blanket snugly around Grandfather, then refilled his teacup.

"All right, all right, Muriel, stop acting like a mother hen. I'm sure you'd like to get to work on dinner, especially since we've a guest. Allison can take care of me while you're in the kitchen."

Muriel looked slightly disappointed, then grinned at Allison. "All right, young lady, he's all yours."

Grandfather turned and gave Allison his full attention. "Allison Mercury O'Brian, why in the name of heaven didn't you let me know you were coming?" he asked.

Allison shifted uncomfortably in the deep leather easy chair and studied the pattern of the Oriental carpet beneath her feet. "I was just so excited . . . I guess I forgot."

"Yes, but then why didn't your mother write or telegram me that you were on your way?"

Allison stared into the embers fighting to ignite the log. Muriel had said not to excite him. "Well," she began. "Marsha—I mean Mother—had to go to Istanbul to make a film, and she was in a terrible hurry."

Grandfather nodded. "It doesn't matter. You're here now. You have no idea how happy this makes me. Having you here is like a dream come true. Sometimes I've felt like an old island out here by myself. You know, it's been almost forty years since I left Ireland and all my relatives behind. And now here I am . . . all alone."

"You came here from Ireland?" she asked, pulling a hassock near the couch to be closer to him.

"Aye, left my family back in Kilkee near Donegal—a fishing town on the west coast. We were all fishermen, but those were hard times back then—back in 1909. My brother James was going to join me the next year after I got set up. But he got married that spring—never made it out."

Allison studied this man carefully. She wanted to memorize each character line carved into his old, weathered face. He folded his large hands in his lap. They were a working man's hands. His thick gray hair stuck out in woolly tufts with eyebrows to match, and his eyes reminded her of the sea on a gray, stormy day. They had a faraway look as he continued his story, as though the importance of all this history needed to be passed on to her while there was the opportunity.

"I met my Mercury on the ship coming over. She had hair that flamed in the sun. Couldn't take my eyes off that hair. She was a Dublin lass—married her in New York and brought her out to Oregon with me. I'd heard there was good fishing out west and room for a man to stretch his legs. Never been sorry I came. But I do miss my family at times."

Allison glanced around the well-furnished room. This was not the house of a lowly fisherman. Somewhere along the line, Grandfather had made some money.

"Grandfather, may I call you Grandpa? It's so much friendlier, and, well, I never really had a grandpa . . . not that I can much recall, anyway. Marsha's dad died when I was two, and I never really knew him."

"You bet you can call me Grandpa!" His face lit up when he smiled, warming Allison even more than the crackling fire on the grate. She held her hands over the flickering flames, and for the first time since Nanny Jane had died, she felt at home and safe.

"Well, Allison, are you keeping him in line?" Muriel asked as she lowered a tray onto the mahogany coffee table in front of Grandpa. "Mr. O'Brian, I think you should have your soup in here. It's warmer than the dining room and I'm sure Allison won't mind. And she can have her supper with me and George a little later."

"Certainly," Allison agreed. "I think this is a delightful room."

Two walls of the room were solidly filled with mahogany bookshelves that stretched to the ceiling and bulged with leather-bound books. Gold-embossed titles glowed in the firelight and promised tales of adventure and intrigue. The fireplace wall was solid stone, and a carved mantelpiece housed interesting treasures of all sorts. Allison felt certain each could tell the story of a far-off land. The opposite wall was covered by forest green velveteen drapes trimmed with gold tassels.

Grandpa followed her gaze as he sipped his soup. "Muriel, open those drapes for Allison," he commanded.

Muriel pulled a golden cord and revealed a gigantic bay window with a padded window seat. The fog had lifted just enough to reveal an incredible view of pounding surf and jagged rocks. Allison leaned over into the window seat and peered out. Her head reeled at the sheer drop-off below.

"Grandpa!" she exclaimed. "It looks like there's nothing to hold us up!"

Grandpa laughed. "I promise you, lassie, we'll not fall into the sea." Allison looked at him doubtfully. "Now, don't worry, my dear, this house is founded on solid rock. It's been sitting here for over sixty years, and I don't expect it to tumble now."

Far to the right she could barely see the beam from the lighthouse. She watched the huge breakers explode onto the rocks below in tall bursts of spray. It looked frightfully beautiful. Allison turned from the breathtaking scene back to the security of the fireplace. The serenity of the beautiful woman in the portrait captivated her.

"What was she like, Grandpa? Mercury, I mean."

Grandpa finished his last bite and folded his hands thoughtfully. "When I met her she was hardly older than you. Sixteen . . . can you imagine sending a pretty sixteen-year-old lassie across the ocean all by herself?"

Allison could have commented on the irony of that statement, but she said nothing—just listened.

Grandpa's gaze seemed to reach far beyond the portrait as he continued. "All she had was a letter from a second cousin in New York to set her up. I noticed her first thing and said to myself, 'Here's a bonnie lassie that needs looking out for.' And that's exactly what I did. Good thing, too, for there were others had their eye on her. But I was a big, strappin' lad and no one tangled with me."

Allison could just imagine him taking on the whole crew to defend the honor of the beautiful Mercury. She wondered when her grandmother had passed on but was afraid to stir up unhappy memories. Marsha had kept so many secrets from her!

"We were married in New York and came straight out to Oregon, poorer than church mice, we were. Mercury had Jamie the following year. Two years later she had little Katherine. But baby Katy died late spring of 1914, the very same day World War I began. Odd . . ."

"And then you lost my father in World War II . . . how tragic."

Grandpa didn't answer. Allison instantly wished she could retract her words. She wanted to cheer him up, not depress him.

"Grandpa, I've always wondered about the name Mercury. I never knew it was my grandmother's name. But why did her parents name her Mercury?"

Grandpa chuckled. "Your grandmother never cared for the name, either. In fact, when I met her she went by Victoria. But when we completed our papers at immigration, I heard them call her Mercury and thought it was perfect. Maybe it was the hair. I called her Mercury ever since. Seems her father wanted to be an astronomer, but he was only a factory worker. He named his first son Jupiter. Then came Mercury. She had another sister, Venus, and I guess the mother put her foot down when the fourth son was going to be named Pluto." Allison laughed.

"I hate to break it up, but I think we should get Mr. O'Brian to his room," Muriel said, breezing into the room with a bottle of medication. "And Dr. Hartley said to take one of these pills at six."

Allison helped Muriel guide Grandpa slowly up the stairs. "Now, you two just let me be. I can get myself up these stairs," he grumbled. "I swear, Muriel just treats me like a child sometimes." Muriel nodded to Allison and smiled knowingly.

Allison sat by his bedside for a few minutes until the medication took effect. "Grandpa, I'm so happy to be here. I'm so glad to finally know you." Tears slid down her cheeks as she leaned over and hugged the sick old man. In her heart she cried, *Please don't leave me. Please, please don't die before I even get a chance to know you. . . .*

 Eight

THE EVEN BREATHING should have assured Allison that Grandpa only slept, but she touched him just to be certain. Still warm. She kept her hand on his weathered one for a moment, noting it was still dirty from planting the tree. She forced herself to rise and, shivering, tossed another small log onto the fire. Was the end of June always this cool in Oregon? She adjusted the blinds, pulled the thick wool coverlet up to his chin, and whispered, "I love you." The words sounded strange, but she meant them with her whole heart.

The walls in the hallway were stark white, and her heels sounded loudly on the hard wooden floor. Many closed doors lined the hall, and Allison tried to imagine which room might've been her father's. It amazed her to think he had actually lived in this house . . . walked down this hall. Had he laughed and played as a little boy? Did he have a favorite hiding place in these silent halls?

The wide stairway was carpeted with a rich jewel-toned runner secured by brass rods on each step. Her hand glided down the polished banister, and she wondered how many others had done the same. Had her father ever slid down this banister? It looked like a good one for sliding.

"Allison, dear," called Muriel from the kitchen.

"Coming," she answered and followed the sound of the voice down another hallway and to the left. The kitchen was like entering another world. It was bright and cheery and well lit. Not that Grandpa's house was completely somber, but it did seem rather serious.

"Allison," Muriel began, "George—that's my husband and

your grandfather's handyman, grounds keeper, chauffeur—you know, the whole bit. Anyway, George just told me he spotted some suitcases out in the bushes by the road. Wouldn't belong to you by any chance?" Muriel cocked her head.

"Holy cow!" exclaimed Allison. "I forgot all about them. I'm glad they weren't stolen."

"I thought so. I told George to bring them up. He's been running some errands in town. Actually, I think he just goes in to gossip with the boys, but I don't let on. Did Mr. O'Brian fall asleep already?"

"Yes, it was a little cool in his room, so I put some more wood on the fire." Allison peeked into the shiny copper pot simmering on the stove. "Mmm, looks good—and warm. Is this house heated only by fireplaces?"

"Oh my, dear, no. But George tries not to run the furnace in the summer months. It's a little cooler than usual this year. Maybe I'll have him start it up, what with Mr. O'Brian's health and all. Here comes Georgie now." Through the back door came what appeared to be walking luggage. Underneath was a stocky little man no taller than Allison.

"Here, let me help you." Allison removed the two smaller bags to uncover a sweet face and a shiny bald head that reminded her of Dopey in *Snow White*.

"Where we puttin' Miss O'Brian?" George asked.

"Up in Katy's room . . . well, of course it's not Katy's room anymore." Muriel glanced at Allison. "George and me just still call it that. You know we've been with Mr. O'Brian for thirty-some years. Can you believe it, Georgie—seems like only yesterday."

Allison followed him up the stairs, glad that he didn't resent her help. He opened the door slowly, almost reverently. She didn't quite know what to expect. Hopefully it wasn't a baby nursery with all the sad mementos of a lost child. But when George turned on the light, she was welcomed by cheery blue-

and-white-striped wallpaper with little yellow rosebuds. On the floor lay a thick area carpet patterned with more yellow roses and soft blue bows. The bed was draped in a pretty patchwork quilt that looked as if it were made to go with the room. Bookcases the color of buttercups surrounded the window and made a little window seat padded in blue velvet. She stared in amazement. If she could have dreamed up a perfect room, it couldn't have been better than this. Yellow was her favorite color. Just as they placed her bags by the door, Muriel called them to supper. Allison had a difficult time leaving the wonderful room but didn't want to keep them waiting.

"I hope you don't mind eating in the kitchen." Muriel scooped a heaping portion of chowder into a bowl and sliced off a hunk of steaming bread.

Allison's mouth watered in anticipation. "Of course not. I like it in here. It's homey and cheerful."

"And warm," George added.

Allison picked up her spoon and was about to take a bite when the old couple bowed their heads. She quickly laid down her spoon and bowed her head with them.

"For that which we are about to receive, may God make us truly grateful. And thank you for getting Miss Allison to us safely. Amen," George mumbled quietly but with sincerity. "Try some of this jam, Allison," he encouraged. "Muriel makes it out of wild strawberries. Last year's, but tasty just the same."

"Dinner's not much tonight. Sunday nights we usually eat light," Muriel explained as she passed her the butter.

"No, it's scrumptious! Much better than train food."

They smiled and George jabbed Muriel lightly with his elbow. "Oh, Muriel's just the best cook in Tamaqua Point and she knows it. She's had lots of offers for other jobs. 'Course, she turns 'em all down. We're happy with Mr. O'Brian—he's like family to us."

After dinner Allison begged Muriel to let her help with the

dishes. Muriel made a fuss but finally gave in.

"These are such pretty dishes," Allison remarked as she dried a glossy blue-and-white willow plate.

"Yes, they were your grandmother's favorites, and over the years I've only broken one teacup and a fruit dish." Allison stacked them carefully, not willing to alter that record.

"The room I'm in upstairs is so lovely, Muriel. You mentioned it was Katy's room, but it doesn't look a bit babyish."

"Oh no, of course not. Mrs. O'Brian decorated it just shortly before she passed on."

Allison stacked the last bowl in the big oak cupboard and closed the door. She could tell by Muriel's voice that Grandmother had been special to her.

"I'll come up with you to freshen your linens. George is fixing you a fire." Muriel picked up some sheets and towels on their way up.

"What's that nice smell?" Allison asked. "This linen closet reminds me of a fresh summer's day."

"Oh, it's lavender," Muriel explained. "Mrs. O'Brian always cut big bunches of fresh lavender from her garden in August to make sachets for the closets and drawers. Even though she's been gone for years, it's a habit I never grow weary of. The smell always reminds me of her."

Allison breathed in the fragrance. She had a strong suspicion she and Grandmother would have gotten along well.

A small fire crackled and snapped in the little fireplace. It was framed in friendly blue-and-white tiles that reminded Allison of her grandmother's pretty dishes. Muriel changed the sheets and freshened the towels in short time, then hesitated by the door.

"Muriel, I know you're probably busy, but I have so many questions. . . ."

"I was hoping you'd ask, darling. Why don't you unpack a

bit and get comfy, and I'll be back up later with a pot of cocoa and we can chat some."

Allison shook out the suits she'd worn on the train and hung them in the closet. It also smelled of lavender. As she placed some sweaters in the top drawer of the oak dresser, she discovered an envelope. It was yellowed with age, and her name, Allison Mercury O'Brian, was written in beautiful lacy handwriting that reminded her of a fancy doily. It had to be from Grandmother! Careful so as not to ruin the envelope, she opened it and slowly read.

June 16, 1942
Dearest sweet Allison,

You may never read this letter, but for now I will pretend that you shall. I have never met you, my dear, and I fear I may never have the pleasure. I know you are eight years old, and I've been told you look a bit like your father, my dear, sweet Jamie. He loves you so. If you never hear it from anyone but me, you must know he loves you. He would be with you if it were possible, but sometimes things happen that we have no control over. I have fixed up baby Katherine's room for you in hopes that you would be able to join us this summer, but it seems it is not to be. Please know this, dear Allison, you are loved. You are an O'Brian. And you will always have a home with us.

Your loving grandmother,
Mercury Victoria O'Brian

A silent tear slid down her cheek. Why had no one told her about this dear grandmother before? Why hadn't they allowed her to visit? A soft tap at the door startled her, and she wiped her wet face with the back of her hands and opened the door.

"I see you found your letter." Muriel opened the drawer of the little bedside table and retrieved a white linen hanky trimmed in hand-tatted lace. "Here's something else for you.

Your grandmother made this from Irish linen." She handed it to Allison. "Many a time over the years I've picked up that letter and dusted around it, wondering if . . ."

Muriel placed the tray on a little table by the fireplace and hugged Allison. "It's all right, dearie, you go ahead and have yourself a good cry. If need be, I might even join you. This family has had more than its share of tragedy, that's for sure."

Allison wept until she had no tears left. She wiped her eyes and took a deep, shuddering breath. They sat quietly beside the crackling fire, Muriel in the overstuffed chair and Allison in the petite sewing rocker.

Allison sipped her cocoa. "I just don't understand Marsha's family. They must've hated my father. I would have absolutely loved to come out here for a visit—and I never even got the chance. I never even knew they existed. Probably never would have, either, if I hadn't taken matters into my own hands."

Muriel nodded. "So your mother doesn't know. Well, I'm not surprised. Now, don't tell anyone, but I'm glad you came. But how in the world did you manage? Do they know where you are? Will we have the police after us? Not that I couldn't take care of them." Muriel grinned.

Allison filled Muriel in on all the details of her trip, and Muriel giggled like a schoolgirl. Allison leaned back in the rocker and warmed her toes by the fire.

"Muriel, this room is so perfect. I've never been in a room that made me feel so special . . . so loved. I feel right at home here."

Muriel's eyes grew misty. "I only hope the saints in heaven can look down from time to time. Your dear grandmother spent the spring of '42 working on this entire room just for you. She fretted over each tiny detail, wanting it to be just right. She ordered the wallpaper from New York—it was pre-war Czechoslovakian, hand printed. The rug came from an expensive catalog, and the bedspread was made by her church's quilting circle.

Mrs. O'Brian knew you'd been sent to boarding school, and she was madder than a wet bee about it. She wanted to keep you here and take care of you for Jamie—until he returned from the war. You can't imagine her disappointment when she got that horrible letter from the Madisons."

Allison leaned over, eyes wide. "What was it about?"

"Oh, it was from your other grandmother. She said awful things about Jamie—just awful! And she told dear Mrs. O'Brian that she would never, never allow you to visit. It broke her heart, it did. I suppose it was no surprise when she became so ill that fall." Muriel twisted her handkerchief and stared into the fire. "After the bad news about Jamie, Mr. and Mrs. O'Brian began to argue. They had never argued before—at least nothing serious. Mrs. O'Brian refused to believe the news about Jamie, but Mr. O'Brian wrote back East demanding proof. Before long, newspaper clippings were sent." Muriel blew her nose loudly. "It was pitiful. Truly pitiful." Allison sat on the edge of her chair waiting for her to continue.

"I'm probably telling too much, but it's nothing you shouldn't know already. Finally poor, stubborn Mr. O'Brian realized that Mrs. O'Brian's health was too far gone. In the end, he even pretended to agree with her about Jamie's innocence—he tried everything to rouse her, but it was too late. She slipped away, leaving Mr. O'Brian like a lost little boy. Took him a long time to get over it, and ever since he's blamed poor Jamie for her death."

Muriel pushed herself up from the chair. "But now you're here, dear. Like a breath of sunshine, you are. Just what the doctor ordered." She stooped to pick up a small pile of laundry that Allison had accumulated on the trip.

"Muriel, I can take care of that. Really, I don't expect you to wait on me."

"We'll have to get one thing straight, young lady. I am paid to work, and besides, I like doing laundry. I don't mind you help-

ing out once in a while, but don't forget who runs this house."
Muriel's smile softened her words.

"Thanks, Muriel. For everything."

"It's late, dear, and I'm sure you must be very tired."

"Do you think Grandpa's feeling better?" She wanted to believe that he would be okay. The reality of his fragile health hit her once again and sent a chill right through her. She still barely knew him. He had to get better. He had to.

"I'm sure he's going to make a miraculous recovery, Allison. He's got such a strong will, and what with you here . . ."

Allison smiled. Of course Muriel had to be right; she'd known Grandpa for years. "Do you think he'd mind if I borrowed a book from his library? I know I won't be able to sleep. I still feel worried, and so much is running through my head."

"Certainly. I know he'll want you to make yourself right at home. I'm going to check on him right now. And George and I will take turns during the night."

"Oh, can I help, too?" Allison asked.

"No, dear. I think what you need is a good night's rest. You'll have the whole day tomorrow to spend with him. By the way, anything you find in this room is for you. This is your room, Allison. It's the way Mrs. O'Brian always meant it to be." Muriel closed the door gently behind her.

Allison looked around the room again. This was *her* room! Not just a pretty spare room, but her very own room. There were a few books on the bookshelf. *A Child's Garden of Verse*, some Beatrix Potter and Winnie the Pooh . . . a little young perhaps, but sweet. She'd have been delighted with them when she was eight. She went to the dainty oak bedside table. It was draped with a delicate crocheted dresser scarf. Allison switched on the sweet little bed lamp, and the pale yellow shade glowed like sunshine. She opened the drawer and discovered a small Bible bound in white leather. Inside, she found the same lacy handwriting dedicating it to Allison from Grandmother. She pressed her lips together and clutched it to her chest. It was a bitter-sweet joy. Someone had really truly loved her even though they'd never met.

Allison pondered her grandmother's sorrow. Perhaps in one way it was fortunate she'd died in the fall of '42, because it was only shortly after that her father was killed in the war. Poor Grandmother, at least she didn't have to face her son's death, too. But Allison's heart ached just the same. Why couldn't things have been different? And why had Grandpa blamed his son for Grandmother's death? It just didn't seem fair. So much sadness. Would she ever get it all sorted out in her head? At least now she had Grandpa. She would get to know him, and maybe in time it would all make sense.

She slipped down to the den to look for a book. The light still shone on Grandmother's portrait. She stared at the lovely woman again. This time she realized that Grandmother Mercury was no longer a stranger. In fact, Allison already felt she knew Grandmother Mercury even better than she knew Marsha.

She explored the shelves and finally settled on a slightly worn volume of *Gone With the Wind*. A lot of her friends had read it at school, but it had always looked so thick she'd shied from it. She'd probably have more time for reading now, and she needed something to keep her mind from fretting. She settled back into her room, but the excitement of the day caught up with her. She was asleep within minutes—deep in the South with hoop skirts swaying and jasmine in the air.

❧   ❧   ❧

The next morning she awoke relaxed and refreshed. The sunshine-filled room greeted her cheerily. A delicious smell wafted from the kitchen, and Muriel met Allison in the hallway with a laden breakfast tray.

"What are you doing up so bright and early? I was just bringing up your breakfast. You won't even let me spoil you for a day!"

"I'm sorry," Allison laughed. "Do you want me to go put on my nightie and jump back into bed?"

"No, but maybe you'd like to take your tray in and join your grandfather for breakfast. He's complaining something terrible about having to stay in bed this morning."

Allison grinned and took the tray from Muriel, then knocked lightly on her grandpa's door.

"Who is it?" he grumbled.

"It's me, Grandpa, may I join you?"

"I should say so," he commanded, his smiling face betraying the warmth behind his gruff voice. "You come right in, Allison. If they're going to lock me in my room, I should at least have some good company, don't you think?"

She rolled a tea cart next to his bed and set her tray down. Then she settled into a nearby overstuffed easy chair. The drapes were drawn, exposing rows of sparkling leaded-glass windows that framed a magnificent view of the ocean. "Grandpa, this room is splendid!"

"Well, it's only fair if I'm to be imprisoned, I should at least enjoy the view."

"And it's beautiful out, not a bit of fog today!" she exclaimed. She took a bite of crispy bacon and spread jam on a biscuit. "Now it even looks like summer."

"If you look over to the left, you can see a fishing rig out there. It's a good day for it. When I'm feeling better maybe we can go out. I've got a friend with a bonnie boat."

"Oh, that would be great. Is it okay with Dr. Hartley?"

"That old horse doctor! What does he know, anyway?"

"Grandpa." Allison tried to sound stern. "I want you to take care of yourself, do you understand?"

He chuckled. "I guess Muriel's right about you. You just might be able to keep me in line."

She noticed a brass telescope set up by the window. "Does that really work?"

"Sure does. Bring it over here and we'll have a look-see."

She set it up close to his bed, and he leaned over and peered out, making some adjustments. "There, now, Allison, look out— just as it is—hurry, now."

"Wow, Grandpa, I can see the men on the boat and nets and lines and everything." She watched for a long time, slowly moving the telescope to follow the fishing rig. She wondered if they knew they were being spied on.

"Yep, I remember that first year here in Oregon. I signed on with the local fishing fleet. Big outfit. Worked my way right up to first mate by the second month. Seems all my years of fishing with my dad off the shores of Ireland finally paid off. I showed them techniques we'd devised back home, and these Oregon waters were just brimming with fish." He sipped his tea and looked across the blue depths of the ocean. "In no time, Hank Jenson offered me a share in the fleet. Maybe he was afraid I'd go into competition with him, but I wouldn't have. Hank was a good man. Things were going well for us. We bought a little cottage after Jamie came. But Mercury worried about me getting lost at sea, and the hours were horrible. I'd read about a need for lumber in California and noticed there was plenty around here. Hank and I talked and talked . . . finally we decided to venture out. That was the birth of the J and O Lumber Shipping Company, back in 1912. I invested what little savings I had and Hank financed the rest. But I was the brains in the operation. I did my research, hunted for the best deals, and it all began to play out just like I'd predicted."

"That must've been exciting! You'd only been in America a few years and you already owned your own business."

"Yep, things were moving along fine when we bought this house in 1913 from an old sea captain. But the next summer little Katherine died, and the war slowed down business. Hank and I even went back to fishing for a while just to make ends meet. Those were rough days. . . . But after the war things picked up again. We couldn't seem to ship lumber fast enough. We bought us another ship and I named her the *Mercury Victoria*. Hank liked the name—he said maybe the Mercury part would make it go faster."

Allison smiled. It was almost like having a ship named after her. Maybe she could see it someday.

"Things went smoothly for a few years, and we were making money hand over fist. Then in 1925 the *Mercury Victoria* shipwrecked during a nasty storm. It was right here at Tamaqua Point. They were heading in for the bay after a long trip from San Diego when they hit the rocks out there. Just smashed the boat to bits—pieces of ship washed up for weeks. Hank was aboard. Some of the crew managed to swim to shore, but not old Hank. . . ." Grandpa's eyes grew misty.

"Oh, Grandpa, I'm so sorry." It seemed a feeble thing to say, but no other words of comfort came to her.

"I'd tried to talk Hank into constructing a lighthouse many a time, but he never thought it was necessary. I handled Hank's share of the business. Of course, he left a monthly stipend for his widow, Beatrice Jenson. With the loss of the ship, we decided to incorporate the business. We sold shares and made enough to replace the ship as well as build a lighthouse. It's named Jenson Light after Hank. But some folks call it the Tamaqua Lighthouse. The government took over the lighthouse during the war, but they put me in charge. I was also the head of the Citizens' Coast Watch. We kept a lookout for Japanese ships, subs, and aircraft."

"That must've been exciting. Did you ever spot anything?"

"No, not really. I thought I saw a submarine once, and even reported it. But later I wondered if it'd been my imagination."

"I think I saw the lighthouse yesterday, but it was so foggy I could only see the beam. I want to see it up close sometime.

Maybe when you're feeling better?"

"I don't think so, Allison. It's hard to get to, and the keeper isn't very friendly. Some people around these parts call him the mad lighthouse keeper."

"Really? Do you think it's true? If he's mad why don't you get rid of him?"

Grandpa's face twisted. "It's not that simple. . . ."

"Are you okay, Grandpa? Am I wearing you out?"

"No, not at all, lassie."

"How was the lighthouse built—I mean, wouldn't it be difficult being on an island?"

"Aye, it was. We took out a crew of six men and a bunch of supplies. Periodically we delivered food and materials. The lighthouse was finally completed the summer of 1928."

"That's exactly twenty years ago! You should have a celebration or something."

Grandpa laughed. "Hmm, we'll see. . . ."

 Nine

AFTER ALLISON HELPED MURIEL with the lunch dishes, she decided to venture down to the shore. Muriel told her about a nice little strip of beach below the house. Because Grandpa had spent the morning entertaining her with tales of days gone by, Allison knew he was due for a rest.

George showed her the way to the steep rock stairs carved into the side of the bluff. "Now, you be careful. On wet days these steps can get pretty slick."

She stepped cautiously on the smooth stones, but they were dry and seemed safe. It was hard to envision a beach below; all she could see were jagged rocks piled on top of one another. The steps wound around and almost under the cliff, emptying out into a protected corner surrounded by rock. And there, sure enough, lay a secluded strip of beach about half a mile long.

The clean white sand was warm from the sun, and she immediately kicked off her shoes and rolled up her pant legs. The water was ice-cold, but she waded in up to her ankles. The sky was cloudless and bluer than a robin's egg. She ran along the water's edge, leaping and splashing until she came to a huge piece of twisted driftwood. She sat on the surf-polished wood and allowed the repetitive sound of the waves to mesmerize her, the only interruption an occasional lonely screech of a sea gull.

And yet another sound teased her ears. Fleeting notes of . . . Was it actually music or just her imagination? She strained her ears to hear. It floated—then vanished. Maybe it was the wind whistling through the cliff rocks. She slid off the log and moved toward the rocks. The notes became clearer, and it sounded like a flute.

Around the corner, seated on a large, flat rock, was a girl with long blond curls that glistened like gold in the sunlight. Though the girl's back was turned, Allison caught the gleam of a silver flute in her hands. Allison blinked at the image before her. It was almost dreamlike, the music ethereal. When she stepped closer she almost expected it to vanish. Then the music ceased. The spell was broken and Allison felt like an intruder.

"Hello," the girl called without turning around.

Allison approached timidly. "Hello? I'm sorry if I disturbed you, but your music was so enchanting. I thought I'd discovered a sea fairy."

The girl laughed. Even her laughter sounded musical; soft and tinkling. She turned and smiled brightly, but her dark, wire-rimmed sunglasses quickly dispelled the fairy image. Allison was relieved to see she was just a normal girl.

"Come on over," said the girl. "I'm Heather Amberwell. I live up on the bluff over there." Allison recognized Heather's British accent. It reminded her of Nanny Jane's, only different.

"I'm Allison O'Brian. And I live—well, actually, I'm staying over there on the other side of the bluff with Mr. Riley O'Brian. Maybe you know him?"

"Oh yes. He's good friends with Grace. Is he a relative?"

"My grandfather. Who's Grace?" Allison asked, hoping she wasn't being nosy.

"Grace Sanders. She's kind of like our mum. Winston calls her Mummy—that's my little brother. He's only nine and he was so little when we lost our parents, he thinks of Grace as his mum."

Allison watched Heather finger the smooth surface of her flute. Allison wanted to ask her dozens of questions, but that might be impolite. "I've only just come to Oregon. Have you been here long? I can tell by your accent you're not from around here."

"No, we came over during the war in '44. Grace brought us.

Our parents were killed in the London bombings. We'd been living in the countryside with a farm family. Grace stayed at the same place and helped care for us. After our parents died, no relatives wanted to take all three of us together. We couldn't bear to be separated, so Grace offered and that's how we came here."

"You say three. You, Winston, and who else?"

"My big brother, Andrew. He's sixteen and he thinks he's the man of the family. Well, in a way he is. You see, Grace's husband was an Air Force officer over there, but he never made it back. He was shot down over France."

"That's too bad. My father died in the war, too."

"I'm sorry. War's a miserable thing. At one time I thought I'd never be happy again, but here I am, just glad to be alive."

"I could hear that in your music. You play beautifully, Heather."

"Thank you. It was my mum's flute. I was only seven when they died, and I'd just begun to play. Now I can't seem to not play."

"And this is just the right spot for it. The sounds go perfect with a day like today."

"How old are you, Allison?" Heather asked abruptly.

"Fourteen."

"Just what I thought. I turn fourteen on Saturday. We're planning a picnic birthday. Maybe you could come?"

"Oh, I don't know. I mean, it sounds great, but I'll have to check with my grandpa. He's been ill, you know."

"Of course. I understand. Do you know what time it is?" Heather pushed a windswept curl from her face.

"Half past two. Goodness, where'd the time go?"

"I thought so. Andrew was supposed to get me at two."

"Why's that?" Allison asked.

Heather looked down and scooped up a fistful of clean white sand. Allison watched the grains slip between her fingers, trickling down like miniature fountains, sparkling in the sunlight.

"Sometimes I use a line on the cliff steps, but today I came with Andrew. He went to do work on something, but he promised to get me at two." Heather faced Allison. "I'm blind."

Allison was speechless.

"It's no big thing, really. I hope it doesn't make you uncomfortable. I've been blind since birth, so I'm used to it."

"I never knew anyone who was . . . blind. It's kind of surprising. I mean, you seem so normal . . . not that you're not normal. I mean—how do you play the flute so beautifully?" Allison felt like she was stumbling all over her words. She was glad Heather couldn't see how red her face was.

Heather laughed again, this time more loudly. "Oh, Allison, it's all right. You'll get used to it. And I play the flute by ear, not by reading music. Though I do read. I love to read, but Braille books are hard to come by."

"I think it's interesting. I can't imagine what it would feel like to not see."

"And I can't imagine what it would feel like to see." They both laughed this time. "Allison, maybe you could help me find my way back home. I really think I could make it, but I got lost once and Grace made me promise to always have someone with me or take the line."

"What's the line?"

"Oh, Andrew rigged it up. He's so inventive. It's just a rope tied to the steps, and I carry it on the beach with me and follow it back. Simple as pie."

Allison had no problem guiding Heather home. The wooden stairs led them straight into a neat little yard. An attractive woman in coveralls with a bandanna on her head met them. She wiped dust off one hand and extended it to Allison.

"I'm Grace," she said pleasantly. "Excuse my appearance, we're doing some fix-ups."

"This is Allison," Heather said. "I found her on the beach. Well, actually, she found me. I'd probably be down there all day if she hadn't come. Andrew promised to get me at two."

"Oh dear, I'm sorry. It's my fault. I sent the boys to town for more paint. I told Andy I'd get you, and I must've lost track of the time."

"Well, Grace, since it was you—and you're nearly perfect— I guess I'll forgive you this time," Heather joked.

"Would you girls like a root beer for your troubles?" Grace offered. "I know I could use one." She stuffed a chestnut curl back into her bandanna.

Allison sat with Heather on the old wooden porch.

"I hear the jalopy," Heather called. "Better bring two more, Grace."

Allison peered down the drive, and sure enough, there came an old red flatbed around the turn. It pulled to the side, and out hopped a young boy in overalls with a curly mop of blond curls. A tall, dark-haired young man reached over the wooden sideboards of the truck and pulled out two big cans of paint.

"Grace, I hope gooseberry green will do, because they were all out of gray," he yelled toward the house.

Grace stepped out with a tray of root beer mugs. "You better be joking, Andy, or one of these drinks will go right down your back."

"Joking, Grace. Only joking." He strode up the stairs in one easy step, stopping abruptly when he saw Allison.

"I didn't know we had a guest." He feigned a dramatic bow.

"This is my nutty brother Andrew, Allison. And this is my new friend, Allison, so be nice. She found me deserted on the beach and rescued me."

"Uh-oh, did Grace forget you? Well, Allison, to you we are eternally grateful," he said dramatically.

They laughed and joked and drank root beer. Winston told them in graphic detail about the dead skunk he saw in the road.

"Ugh, and on that note, I think I better go. Thanks for the story, Winston. I shall remember it always," Allison said.

"Oh, must you go so soon?" Heather looked genuinely disappointed. "You see, Winston, you scared my new friend away."

Winston looked truly sorry.

"No, you didn't," laughed Allison. "It's just that my grandpa is ill and I don't want to be gone too long."

"Well, how about my party? Grace, I invited Allison to join us. I knew you wouldn't mind. What time shall we say?"

"I thought around ten on Saturday morning. We'll drive up to Arrowhead Rock."

"I'll have to see. It'll depend on my grandpa's health. Can I call you later?"

"I'll write down the number for her," Andrew offered.

"I'm sorry, I don't know my grandpa's number. But it's the O'Brian place."

"You mean Riley O'Brian?" Grace asked in surprise.

Allison nodded. "He's my grandpa," she said with pride.

"Of course . . . just look at you!" Grace exclaimed. "You are James O'Brian's daughter!" She swayed slightly and her face grew pale.

"Are you all right, Grace?" Andrew asked, easing her into the big wicker chair. "You look like you just saw a ghost."

"I sort of feel that way. . . ." Grace stared at Allison in disbelief, then reached out and touched her shoulder. "I'm so sorry, dear. It's just that when I met you, you felt so familiar to me— but I couldn't put my finger on it. Now it's as plain as day. You're your father's daughter."

Allison's breath caught in her throat. "You mean you knew my dad?"

"Knew him well," Grace nodded. She looked out past the porch in a faraway stare. "Knew him very well. He was a good man."

Allison glanced nervously at her watch. She longed to stay

and find out more, but she knew she had to get back to Grandpa. Already she'd been gone much longer than she'd intended. "Well, I guess we'll have to talk more later. Thanks for everything. I'll call you, Heather—about the party."

She dashed up the beach. A thick bank of fog crept in off the horizon. She hoped Grandpa was okay. Why had she stayed away so long? She ran until she came to the steps and remembered the warning. Climbing carefully, it seemed to take forever to reach the top. In the yard, George was busily planting another tree. He waved as she dashed for the kitchen door.

"Allison!" Muriel exclaimed. "What a fright you gave me. What's the great hurry?"

"I . . . I didn't mean to spend so much time away, and I just got so worried about Grandpa," she explained breathlessly. "Is he okay?"

"Oh, darling, now, don't you fret. He just woke up from a nap and is looking ever so much better. I was about to take some tea up for him. If you could slow down long enough, maybe you could take it for me."

"Sure, just let me wash up a bit first."

Grandpa was perched up in his bed amidst a stack of pillows when Allison entered his room a few minutes later. He glanced up, dropped his book on his lap, and stretched out his hand to her. "Come in here, lassie. Now, you're looking fine. You've got roses in your cheeks and a sparkle in your eye."

"I was about to say the same to you." She set the tray down.

"Then I see our beach agrees with you. I always knew you'd love it here. I'm just so glad you finally came."

"Grandpa, I do love it here. I feel so at home. I even made friends already."

Riley's eyebrows arched. "Who would that be, my dear?"

"I met a lovely girl out on the beach. Her name is Heather."

"Oh, one of Grace's gang," he smiled. "Nice folks."

"Yes, and Saturday is Heather's birthday. She asked me to

join them on a picnic, but I told them it would depend on you."

"Of course you'll go! You can't let an old codger like me slow you down. After all, this is your vacation. I can't hog all your time. I haven't asked yet—I'm almost afraid to—but I have to know. How long are they letting you stay? I know it wasn't an easy thing for them to allow you to come. . . ."

Allison looked out the window at the fog bank slowly creeping in. Would Marsha even find out? "Oh, Grandpa, I can stay all summer . . . perhaps even longer." The way his face lit up, she didn't care if it wasn't exactly the truth. For now it would have to do.

"This will be the best of summers, then," Grandpa proclaimed.

Allison shared his smile, then paused. "Grandpa, Grace mentioned she knew my dad. I could hardly believe it. There's so much I'd like to know about him."

She watched as he gazed out the window. His face reminded her of the sunshine just as it was doused by the fog. She wished he would talk about her father, especially since he was such a wonderful storyteller. She wondered why he clammed up whenever she brought up the subject. It was almost as if he hated his own son. Did he still, after all these years, blame his son for her grandmother's death? Had her father, a man she'd never known, really been a terrible person?

Ten

GRANDPA AND ALLISON SPENT the following day together. She didn't want to leave his side for a moment. She knew she'd never tire of him and hoped he wouldn't grow weary of her. After dinner Grandpa made a fire in the den fireplace.

"You know the weather isn't always this bad in the summertime. But it is unpredictable, that's for sure," he said.

"Oh, I like days like this, Grandpa. Of course, I wouldn't want them all the time." She examined a German nutcracker on the mantel. "Where did this come from? Have you been to Germany?"

"Do you play chess, Allison?" he asked, changing the subject. He slid the carved marble chess set next to him.

"I'm not much of a player. I mean, I know how to play, but I don't play very well." She replaced the nutcracker. She suspected it had been sent by her dad during the war. Nanny Jane had said he'd been serving in Europe.

"Hmm, well you're an O'Brian, and you come from a long line of chess players, so we better try you out."

Allison scooted a hassock over by the large table and watched Grandpa arrange the pieces. She wondered if her dad had been a chess player, too.

"First we'll just play quick games to warm up on, and I'll give you some pointers and hints, all right?"

Allison nodded and listened as he continued to explain some basic principles of the game. After a couple of short games, Allison found she understood it better and actually liked chess.

"Do you want to play another, Grandpa? I don't want to wear you out." She reset the pieces.

"Are you sure you're up for it? I feel ruthless—I might massacre your chessmen."

"It's okay, Grandpa, I can take it." She grinned. They played for almost an hour.

"By golly, girl. You play just like your fath—" He stopped before the word was out. He stood and stretched, then poked the dying embers in the fireplace. "You're going to be one good chess player, Allison Mercury. But I think I better call it a day. Good night."

"Good night, Grandpa. Thanks for the lessons." Allison replaced the chess pieces and scooted the hassock back. She sat down in front of the fire and warmed her hands. The sound of rain beating against the window made the den seem even cozier than usual.

"Yoo-hoo," Muriel called. "Ah, there you are. Would you like to join me in the kitchen for some tea and shortbread?"

"You made shortbread?" Allison exclaimed. "I love shortbread. Nanny Jane used to make it—she was Scottish."

"You must mean Jane McAllister. I was so sorry to hear of her passing on. She was the one who tipped off Mr. O'Brian to your whereabouts. God rest her soul. . . . This recipe is from Mrs. O'Brian. She enjoyed shortbread and tea."

Muriel poured Allison a cup of tea. "Allison, I hate to bring this up, but I think we should discuss it. Do you have any intentions of letting your folks back East know of your little escapade?"

"I—uh, I don't know. I haven't given it much thought. . . ." Allison hung her head. This was a subject she'd like to forget—forever.

"I know it's not easy, dear. It just concerns me that someone may be worried about you or call the authorities. I'd hate to see you get in trouble."

"I know, I know. . . . Maybe I'll write a letter to my mother and explain what I did. Maybe she'll understand." *Sure,* Allison thought. *That'll be the day.*

"That would make me feel a lot better. I want you to be able to spend as much time here as possible. And if they think we kidnapped you, I'm sure it won't go over well."

"Okay, Muriel. I'll write it tonight," she promised.

Muriel hugged Allison and gave her another piece of short-bread.

Later that night, Allison opened the little writing desk in her room. It was outfitted with stationery and pens. She sat and stared into the blank white sheet. What could she possibly say that would convince Marsha to let her stay?

> *Dear Marsha,*
>
> *I'm sure you will be surprised to learn I'm in Oregon. Yes, I traveled across the country to meet my grandfather. My grandfather, whom I'd never even heard of until this past month. My grandfather, who may be dying.*
>
> *I want to stay here with him. I know I'm only an inconvenience to you. So I am not asking you, Marsha. Let me stay with Grandpa for the rest of his days. If you don't, I will run away. I mean it!*
>
> *Allison*

Tears streamed down her face as she folded the letter and sealed the envelope. She knew Marsha wouldn't like her tactics, but she didn't care. Once and for all, Allison surrendered all hope that Marsha would ever love her. She dried her eyes on the handkerchief left in the dresser. Had Grandmother Mercury known she'd need it?

❧   ❧   ❧

The next day the letter was gone from her desk. She figured Muriel had mailed it but couldn't bring herself to ask. Perhaps it had gotten lost somewhere.

The week seemed to speed by, and Grandpa, ever so slowly, felt better each day. They took brief walks around the yard at first, and as his strength improved they ventured farther. One day they went down a winding little road that led to a floating dock on the inlet. From that side of the bluff, they could see the lighthouse. There it stood, proud and white on the small, rocky island.

"Oh, Grandpa, it's wonderful! I wish we could visit it." Grandpa skipped a stone across the water without saying anything. She wondered if the stories about the lighthouse keeper were bothering him.

"What is it they say that the mad lighthouse keeper does?"

"They're just rumors."

"Do you know him?" Allison asked.

Grandpa turned away, his face gray.

Allison grabbed his arm. "Are you okay? Should we go back to the house?"

"I'm all right. Just a bit tired." He sat down on a stumpy post of the pier and rubbed his forehead as if he was trying to remember something.

Allison picked up a stone and tried to skip it across the water, but it was swallowed by a small wave. She sat down next to him and studied the old but well-cared-for rowboat that was tied securely to the dock. It bobbed up and down with the waves, bumping against the pier in gentle, regular thumps. "Whose dock is this, Grandpa?"

"Mine." He got up and checked the rope on the boat.

"Really? Is this your boat?"

"Aye, my bonnie little boat."

"What do you use it for?"

"I don't use it anymore. The doctor forbids it." He grunted. "Used to take it out to fish and crab, though."

"I wish I could take it out—"

"Allison, I don't want you to ever, ever take it out! Under-

stand?" His voice was so firm it took her by surprise. She nodded mutely.

"I'm sorry," he continued. "I didn't mean to startle you. It's
just that this is a dangerous inlet. You must know the tides and
how to handle a boat."

Allison understood. She knew about inlets and tides from
sailing in Massachusetts but decided not to bring it up. No need
to worry or upset him. She looked again at the lighthouse. It
seemed so small. How could someone actually live inside?
Maybe that's why he was mad.

She turned to Grandpa. "Don't you think we should throw
Jenson Light a birthday party? Twenty years old is quite a mile-
stone, you know, even for a lighthouse. Happy birthday, lighthouse!" she yelled across the inlet.

Grandpa laughed. "Speaking of birthdays, didn't you mention Heather invited you for a picnic on Saturday?"

"I almost forgot! I never even called her back."

"Don't worry, it's not too late. Why don't we head back and
you can call."

As they made their way back to the house, Allison decided
to try some new tactics to get her grandfather to open up. If he
wouldn't discuss her father, maybe she could find something
out about Grace and her connection to this mystery. "Grandpa,
how do you know Grace? She seems like such a lovely person."

"Grace is a truly wonderful person, Allison. She's a local
girl—went to nursing college and then joined the Red Cross
during the war. She was stationed in England where she met
her husband—a dashing Air Force lieutenant, as I understand.
The way I heard the story, when her Red Cross quarters were
destroyed in London, she journeyed with evacuees to the countryside, including the Amberwell children. You probably know
the rest of that story. Anyway, she and her husband were married for less than a year when his plane went down. It was tragic,
but what she's done for those children is remarkable."

Not one word about her dad. It figured.

They passed through the garden. Allison stopped to sniff the rose blooms. "These smell delicious. Try them."

Obligingly, he bent to smell. "Yes, they were Mercury's favorites. Can't remember the name, though. Pick as many as you like, Allison. This garden needs to be enjoyed more. Poor old George slaves away and no one seems to notice. There are some shears in the shed there."

"Thanks, Grandpa."

She peered into the shed. A little window let in just enough light to see the orderly shelves, and there on a hook hung a large pair of shears. As she reached for them she noticed a piece of paper with what appeared to be a list of provisions, including items like beans, flour, and lamp oil. She wondered who would be needing lamp oil. It was signed with what looked like the letter J. Who would that be, and why was it in the shed?

She strolled the garden, pondering this mystery. Who was J? Or was it a J? Maybe it was really a misshapen G for George, or maybe he spelled his name with a J. She finally decided to cut some of Grandmother Mercury's favorite roses to make a pretty pale pink bouquet. She carried them inside and Muriel found a cut crystal vase. Allison took her time arranging the roses until they were just right, then placed her masterpiece on the dining room table.

"This is such a lovely room, Muriel. Not a bit stuffy like some dining rooms I know. . . ." On the walls hung pale yellow-and-cream-striped wallpaper. The mahogany chairs were padded and covered with a pale yellow tapestry, and the giant atrium doors opened out onto a slate terrace surrounded by a garden.

"Yes, Mrs. O'Brian had a way with colors and decorating. And she loved fresh flowers—the garden was one of her favorite places." Muriel opened the doors and let the afternoon sunshine beam in. "She planted those hedges ages ago to protect it from the winds." She motioned to the thick wall of arborvitae. "Still, it took years before she could coax those roses to bloom. But at last the hedges are all filled in and now it's just lovely."

"Say, Muriel, does George spell his name with a *J*?"

"No, with a *G*, dear. Why?"

"Oh, nothing . . ."

"Dinner's at six tonight, Allison. You shall be dining formally, so you may wish to dress up." Muriel said this in a funny tone, then winked at her.

Allison went to her room to clean up. What was Muriel up to? She switched on her little radio, and the smooth voice of Nat King Cole filled her room. George had given her the radio yesterday. She thought about how he'd seemed embarrassed, saying it was just an old junker he'd salvaged and fixed up. But she could tell by the shiny wooden cabinet that it had been carefully cleaned and polished. Even more important, it worked swell.

She glanced at herself in the oak-trimmed mirror above her dresser. It was fun being fourteen again. She wore a grass-stained white jersey that Marsha would no longer recognize, and her watermelon red shorts were wrinkled and dirty. Muriel had said tonight would be a formal dinner. She searched her closet for an appropriate outfit.

She'd packed a mint green dress in case of a formal occasion. She held it up. It didn't really seem to be Marsha's style, and it looked as if it had never been worn. It was very pretty, but maybe too dressy. She held up the peach rayon suit and wondered which one Grandpa would like better. She chose the dress. For some reason she wanted to impress Grandpa tonight. She wanted to make him proud. Her secret hope was that he'd ask her to live with him. She'd hinted at it once, but he hadn't responded. Maybe he didn't want to be saddled down with a teenager at this point in his life, not to mention his poor health. She wanted to make him understand that she was independent and able to look after herself. She wouldn't be any trouble at all.

She studied herself in the mirror as she brushed her hair. Even Grace had said she looked like her father. Maybe Grandpa didn't want to have her around if she reminded him of his son. But then again, he had also said she looked like Grandmother Mercury. And besides, Grandpa truly seemed to love her. She just knew it.

She pinned the mother-of-pearl brooch on the bodice of the satin dress. Now she remembered why she'd bought it for Marsha. Of course she'd thought it was pretty, but when Nanny Jane had said it was made with mother-of-pearl, Allison had misheard her and thought she'd said "mother-of-girl." She'd then imagined it was a magical pin, and once pinned to Marsha, she'd be instantly transformed into a real mother. Allison laughed. She'd been young and naïve then. But somehow, now that Grandpa was in her life, her feelings about Marsha didn't seem so bitter anymore.

Just before six o'clock she ventured down to the den, but Grandpa wasn't there. She heard female voices in the parlor and peeked in to see.

"Allison, come in," Grandpa hailed. "Meet some dear friends of mine. Beatrice Jenson, this is my Allison. And, Allison, meet Bea's granddaughter, Shirley, who's visiting from California."

"How do you do?" Allison said. The elderly woman heartily shook her hand, and the girl nodded slightly from across the room without getting up.

"It's such a pleasure to meet you, Allison. And on such a happy occasion. I hear this was your idea." Mrs. Jenson winked. But Allison had no idea what she meant.

"You see, I took your advice, Allison," Grandpa stated. "We are having an official birthday party for the Jenson Light. And I figured we better invite Bea since it bears her name."

"That's wonderful, Grandpa!" Allison exclaimed.

"Yes, I was so surprised when Riley called me up today. Shirley just came up from California, and we were as pleased as punch to come over."

Bea and Grandpa began reminiscing over the good old days, and Allison felt responsible to draw out the quiet girl on the couch. She sat down across from Shirley and nervously smoothed the satin folds of her skirt.

"Where in California are you from?" she asked. The girl looked to be around sixteen, but it could've been the clothes and makeup. Allison remembered her own charades.

"San Diego. Do you know where that is?" Something about the way Shirley spoke felt like a put-down.

"Well, I've never actually been there, but I can find it on the map," Allison answered brightly. "I'm fourteen. How old are you?"

Shirley rolled her dark eyes, fluttered mascara-enhanced lashes, and sighed deeply. "Fifteen and a half."

Allison studied her. She didn't like to make snap judgments on people, especially friends of Grandpa, but this Shirley definitely got under her skin. What was it about her? She reminded Allison of—*Marsha!*

"Dinner is served," George announced.

Allison stifled a giggle. She'd never seen George dressed so formally. His jacket barely buttoned around his middle, and he resembled Tweedledee . . . or was it Tweedledum? Grandpa took her arm and escorted her into the dining room. The soft glow of candlelight reflected on shining crystal and polished silver. In the center stood her arrangement of roses.

"Everything looks lovely," Allison whispered to Grandpa.

"Not half as lovely as you, lassie," he smiled. "You make me very proud, Allison Mercury." He seated her at the place where the mistress of the table would sit. Never had she felt so important or so loved.

"How long are you staying in Tamaqua Point, Shirley?" Allison asked congenially. She'd just gotten her second wind of graciousness. She imagined her grandmother patiently entertaining a cantankerous visitor.

"The entire summer," Shirley complained. "What do you people do here for entertainment, anyway?"

"Actually, I've only been here a week, but I've enjoyed every minute." Shirley rolled her eyes again. Allison gave up and joined in the adults' conversation.

"Remember that time you and Hank caught the squid and brought it home and put it in my bathtub?" Bea laughed. She had one of those full, hearty laughs that invited everyone to join in. "I went in that evening all ready for a nice soak and there he was! I could have murdered you two!" She laughed so hard tears streamed down her rosy cheeks.

"Dinner is scrumptious, Muriel," Allison commented, wishing Muriel could join them. But Muriel was obviously delighted just to serve up her appetizing dishes.

"Yes, Muriel. You must share your recipe for this seafood salad. Mine isn't half as tasty," Bea complimented.

"And she threw this little party together with only a few hours' notice," Grandpa said with pride.

"I was just wondering how you did this." Allison eyed him suspiciously.

"Well, Bea and I were talking business this morning, and I invited her and Shirley up. When you mentioned a lighthouse birthday, I just figured I'd kill two birds with one stone."

"How complimentary, Riley," Bea joked.

Just then Muriel came in with a white-frosted cake. It faintly resembled the lighthouse and had a ring of candles burning brightly around the top.

"Muriel, it's wonderful!" Allison exclaimed. "We must sing 'Happy Birthday'!" Shirley groaned, but Allison ignored her.

"First, a toast," Bea said, holding up her glass. "To a fine partnership that was only too brief." Tears glistened in the old woman's eyes and her voice grew husky. "To the good times and good memories . . ."

Grandpa continued for her. "And to Hank Jenson, a fine friend, and to the lighthouse that bears his name. Happy birthday, Jenson Light."

George and Muriel joined in and they all sang, except for Shirley, who acted like they were all senile. Bea and Grandpa blew out the candles together.

"Riley, I'm afraid I'm so full from dinner, I couldn't possibly eat another bite," Bea said.

"Why don't we have the cake later," Allison suggested, enjoying her role as hostess. "We could take a walk through the garden. It's so beautiful this time of evening."

They stepped out the atrium doors, and the garden was illuminated by the soft pink glow of the sky. The roses took on colors so vibrant that Allison wished she knew how to paint so she could capture their beauty forever.

"Simply lovely," Bea exclaimed. Shirley slumped along looking only at her feet.

"Hello?" a friendly voice called. "George said you were out here." Heather's brother Andrew strolled up. "I'm terribly sorry to disturb you, but I've come as a messenger to the fair Lady Allison," he proclaimed with dramatic flourish. "Actually, our telephone's on the blink, and Heather sent me over to see if Allison can come on the picnic tomorrow." He looked at Allison, then did a double take and whistled. "You are the same Allison, aren't you?"

"Of course, silly." Allison laughed. She was thankful for the dusky light and hoped no one noticed her blushing cheeks. "I'd love to come. In fact, I tried to phone Heather this afternoon but couldn't get through."

"Then it's settled," Grandpa said. "Now, Andrew, come on in and join us for a piece of birthday cake."

"Another birthday?" Andrew asked.

"Yes, we're celebrating the twentieth birthday of Jenson Light."

"Oh, you mean the Tamaqua Lighthouse," Andrew said.

"I beg your pardon, young man," Bea corrected. "Its official name is the Jenson Light."

"I stand corrected," Andrew said in mock humility but with a genuine smile.

Grandpa slapped him on the back. "Smart man . . . never pays to argue with a woman." He led the small procession back to the house.

They settled in the parlor for cake and tea, and Allison felt Andrew's eyes on her as she took a bite of cake.

"Heather said to tell you to come prepared for anything, sunshine or fog, swimming or hiking. Just don't pack the kitchen sink," Andrew said with a chuckle.

"Swimming?" Shirley exclaimed, stepping up to Andrew and smiling for the first time the entire evening. "I *adore* swimming. Where *does* one go to swim around here?"

Allison could only see the back of Shirley's head, but she could just imagine those dark eyelashes fluttering wildly.

"Uh . . . well, we have a special spot. Maybe I could draw you a map," Andrew offered.

"Poor Shirley," Bea exclaimed. "She's been so deprived of youthful companionship up here. I've been afraid she might just whither away." Allison wondered how poor Andrew would handle that very obvious hint.

"Maybe . . . uh, you'd like to join us tomorrow. It's my sister's fourteenth birthday—"

"I'd simply *love* to. Oh, she's fourteen—just a year younger than I. I'm sure I'll just *love* her."

When Shirley turned on the charm, it really oozed. Allison almost wanted to back out now, but for Heather's sake, she knew she couldn't. Suddenly, it appeared her afternoon with Heather was going to be more of a chore than a party.

Eleven

ALLISON JERKED HER FLANNEL NIGHTGOWN over her head, her pleasant expectations of tomorrow's picnic now squelched. Why must Shirley invade their fun? She stood before her dresser and admired the smooth tortoiseshell comb set left to her by Grandmother Mercury. Muriel had mentioned the set had come from Ireland. As she brushed her hair, she imagined her grandmother braving the Atlantic crossing alone. She looked into the mirror and considered her own cross-country trip. Maybe she was a lot like her grandmother. Well, then, she could be brave enough to face the likes of Shirley Jenson.

Thoughts of Shirley once again reminded Allison of Marsha. The two seemed to be cut from the same cloth. Just her luck after traveling thousands of miles to get away from Marsha's grasp to be yoked with her equal. Maybe she was overreacting. She thought about Andrew—remembering the way he'd looked at her tonight. It was as if he were seeing her for the first time. Had it only been her imagination? She recalled the other boys who'd been in her life only recently. There was John on the train leaving New York, but he'd viewed her like a younger sister. Then there was Mr. O'Conner's son, Mark. He was nice but a little bit boring. And now there was Andrew. His crazy antics, serious green eyes, and handsome face intrigued her. She was certain that behind his mask of wit was a deep and sensitive person. A person she would like to know better.

&c&c &c&c &c&c

The next morning dawned cloudy. *Too bad for Heather*, Allison thought. She pulled on a heavy tweed sweater and corduroy trousers, then she packed some lighter things just in case the weather changed. At the last minute she even threw in a swimsuit.

But what about a birthday present for Heather? She hadn't thought about that. What could she give? She couldn't exactly run down to Macy's. *Macy's!* What had she done with the perfume she'd bought? She pulled the suitcases out of the closet. There, tucked in a deep side pocket, was the small white box. She pulled it out and spotted the letter from Marsha's secret closet. She'd forgotten all about it! She would read it again later and perhaps show it to Grandpa. Or would it only dredge up more bad feelings about her father? What did the letter mean, anyway? Did it have anything to do with what Muriel had said? Allison tucked it back into the suitcase pocket, deciding to figure it out later. Right now the smell of bacon drifted into her room with a promise of breakfast.

"I was just wondering if you were going to get up this morning, Allison," Grandpa teased when she entered the dining room. He sipped his coffee at the big dining room table.

"I was getting something for Heather's birthday." Allison took a swallow of orange juice. "Maybe I'll take her some roses, too, if that's okay."

"You bet! Take her some for me, as well. Heather's such a nice lassie. I'm happy you met her so soon."

"Does she go to school?" Allison asked. "I mean . . . since she's blind."

"You bet she does," Grandpa replied. "Between Grace and the boys, Heather gets around just fine. She's quite an independent gal, considering. We've tried to stock the Tamaqua school with plenty of Braille books. Next year she'll start high school in Port View—I hope she'll do all right there."

"Where's Port View?"

"It's a large town south of here—about twenty miles. All the kids here 'bouts go to Port View High."

"Hellooo?" called a female voice down the hallway. "I knocked but no one answered, so I let myself in."

Allison turned in surprise to see Shirley. She looked like an advertisement for a fashion magazine. Her bright red clam diggers and red-and-white-striped jersey were a bit on the snug side. Her hair was styled high and tied with a red silk scarf that matched her earrings and lipstick. Her perfume preceded her and nearly ruined Allison's breakfast.

"Come on in, Shirley. Care for some coffee or tea?" Grandpa offered.

"I'll take a cup of coffee," Shirley said, plopping down across from Allison. Grandpa picked up the newspaper, and Allison quickly finished up her last piece of toast.

"Excuse me, I'm going out to cut some roses for Heather," Allison said, thankful for a reason to escape her unwanted guest.

"Oh murder! I forgot it's a birthday picnic. Dear Mr. O'Brian, you won't mind if I cut some flowers, too?" Grandpa nodded absently.

Allison glared at Shirley. Why did Shirley have to copy her? Allison forced a smile and held the door open.

Out in the garden, Shirley cut a little of everything, ending up with the wildest bouquet Allison had ever seen. Good thing Heather didn't have to look at it! Allison selected several sweet rosebuds and ran upstairs to get her things.

She glimpsed at her image in the mirror. It looked rather plain in contrast to Shirley's exotic outfit. She shook her head and rolled her eyes, remembering her own days of masquerading in New York. From now on she'd rather be fourteen. She scooped up her bag and skipped down the stairs.

George dropped the two girls off at Grace's and waved goodbye. Winston ran up to Allison but stopped short when he saw Shirley. He eyed her up and down, then turned to Allison.

"I saw a dead porcupine on the road yesterday! It was flatter than a pancake, with blood and everything!" he exclaimed. Allison laughed, while Shirley backed off and gave them both an odd look.

"Come on over here, ladies," Andrew called from the porch. "Shirley, come and meet the rest of the troops."

"Oh, don't you just love his accent," Shirley gushed to Allison. Andrew quickly dispensed with introductions and continued to load the jalopy.

"Heather," Allison whispered. "I have a present for you. Should I give it to you here or wait till later?"

"No time like now!" Heather smiled. She fingered and smelled the dainty rosebuds. "Oh, they're lovely, Allison. I'll bet they're pink."

"How do you know?" Allison gasped.

"I don't know . . . they just smell so pretty and . . . pink." They laughed and Heather ran her fingers over the smooth surface of the box. It was embossed with little flowers. She felt each one in detail. Finally she opened it. Her fingers traced the pear shape of the smooth glass bottle and gently opened the lid. "'Tis marvelous, Allison. It smells just like a meadow of wild flowers."

"Oh, here you go, Heather," Shirley said, holding the flowers a few feet from Heather. "Look, aren't they just gorgeous?"

Heather laughed lightly, and Allison couldn't help but giggle, too.

"What's so funny?" Shirley asked. "I think they look real colorful and pretty. Sorry I didn't have a chance to buy you a nicer present." She stood before the two girls, awkwardly holding her flowers with a puzzled look.

Allison looked up at Shirley's dazzling bright outfit and ridiculous bouquet and burst into uncontrollable fits of laughter.

"I'm sorry, Shirley," Heather apologized between giggles. "It's just that I can't *see* your gift." She exploded, "Because I'm blind!" She and Allison practically rolled off the porch in hysterics. Tears streamed down their cheeks, and Allison thought her sides would burst.

"Real funny! Blind . . . yeah sure!" Shirley muttered in disgust.

"It's true," Andrew said seriously. "But hey, what's the joke with you two?"

Heather and Allison couldn't even speak they were so overcome with hilarity. Allison tried to explain between giggles, and before long their mirth became contagious and Andrew burst out laughing, too. Shirley stood in the yard with an exasperated expression, the flowers hanging limply in her hand.

"All right, you clowns," Grace said. "I think this is the last box." She handed it to Andrew. "It'll be a bit tight, but I think the girls can ride in front and the fellows in back."

Shirley climbed into the truck silently. Allison figured she was in shock. Grace, Heather, and Allison sang songs from the hit parade all the way to Arrowhead Rock.

"Do you know that Bing Crosby one?" Heather asked. "You know, 'Mares eat oats and does eat oats and little lambs eat ivy. . . .' " They sang it until everyone burst into laughter. Everyone but Shirley. She just sat in silence.

"Oh, Heather, the sun decided to show up for your birthday!" Allison exclaimed as they pulled into the parking lot. They carried the picnic supplies to a table near the beach. It was a perfect little cove protected from the wind, with a nice big strip of beach. Out in the water stood a gigantic rock shaped like an arrowhead.

"When the tide's out you can wade right up to the rock, but at high tide you swim out to it and climb up to the top," Heather explained.

"Have you climbed it?" Allison asked.

"Only once. Of course, Andrew helped me." Heather smiled proudly. "Come on, Al, let's get our feet wet." They kicked off their shoes and rolled up their pants. Heather grabbed Allison's hand and together they ran into the surf. Allison relished the feeling of being called Al. It made her feel wanted.

"That Shirley is really something else," Heather commented when they were well out of earshot.

"You said it," Allison replied, marveling at her friend's intuition.

"Andrew admitted he was forced into inviting her." Heather swished her toe through the wave.

"That's about right. Actually, she kind of invited herself."

"She's probably just lonely. I guess we should be nice to her. I feel bad about what happened on the porch, but it just struck me so funny. I'll have to try harder."

Allison decided for Heather's sake she'd make an effort, too. They found a warm bank of sun-baked sand to thaw out their feet.

"You know, Allison, I can tell you exactly what you look like," Heather remarked as she leaned back on the sand.

"Come on, Heather," Allison laughed. "You were right about the roses, but can you describe people, too?"

"Uh-huh. Now, let me think. . . . You have reddish hair, almost auburn, and it glistens in the sun like copper." Allison was amazed. "Your skin is creamy white, sprinkled with a few freckles, just enough to give personality. And you have big brown, no, green—well, now, I'm not sure about the color. But they're pretty eyes—"

"Hey, wait a minute," Allison interrupted. "Grace talked to you!"

Heather laughed with glee. "Had you going, didn't I? But you're wrong . . . it wasn't Grace. It was Andrew."

Allison didn't reply. She wondered if those were Andrew's words or Heather's. It surprised her how much she hoped they were Andrew's. She glanced over her shoulder to see Andrew and Shirley down by the water's edge. Winston was digging in the sand nearby. An unexpected twinge of jealousy shot through Allison.

"Lunchtime!" Grace called. Allison leaped up, grabbed Heather's hand, and they dashed to the table.

"I'm so sorry, Grace," Allison said. "I didn't even offer to help."

"There was nothing to it. It was just a matter of setting everything out." She filled another glass of lemonade. There were deviled eggs, fried chicken, potato salad, rolls, coleslaw, and pickles, all arranged nicely across the red-checkered cloth. They stood around the table, but no one moved for the food. Then Grace grasped Heather's hand on one side and Winston's on the other. Andrew followed suit holding Allison's and Shirley's, and they formed a circle.

"Father in heaven," Grace began. "Thank you for all you've done for us and for this fine day. Thank you for our new friends, Allison and Shirley. Please bless this food. And richly bless Heather as she celebrates her birthday today. Amen."

Allison tried to concentrate on the prayer, but all she could think about was that Andrew was holding her hand. And it distracted her even more to think he was also holding Shirley's. Soon they were all digging in and heaping their plates.

"Everything was too delicious, Grace. I'm incredibly stuffed," Allison moaned as she finished her last bite.

"Heather, come see the neat dead crab I found. He's this big." Winston stretched Heather's arms about a foot apart.

"Are you sure about that, Winston?" Heather asked skeptically. She let him take her by the hand. Andrew wandered off and Shirley trailed after him.

"I'll help you clean up, Grace," Allison offered, trying not to notice how Shirley seemed to be magnetized to Andrew. Instead, she kept herself busy by cleaning up the picnic, and soon the food was all nicely packed away. Heather and Winston were down on the beach, but Andrew and Shirley were nowhere in sight. That bothered Allison some, but the most troublesome part was that it irritated her, too. She hardly even knew Andrew. Why should she care if he wanted to spend time with Shirley? Besides, Allison had come for Heather's sake. And since Heather was occupied, Allison decided this was her chance to find out what Grace might know about her dad.

"Grace," Allison began, "I've been dying to know just how it was that you knew my dad."

Grace shook the food scraps off the plaid woolen blanket and spread it on the sand. She sat down, slipped off her sneakers, and dug her toes into the sand. "Well, Allison, we met in high school and became friends." Grace turned and looked at her. "Just how much do you really want to know?"

"Everything!" Allison demanded with a smile.

"Everything? That might take a while. . . ." Grace sighed and pulled the pretty silk scarf off her head. She ran her fingers through her hair and shook out her shiny chestnut curls.

"Just start at the beginning and we'll see how far you get. We can always take it in stages. And from the looks of things, Grace, you're the only one who's going to tell me anything about my father."

Grace eyed Allison quizzically. "Let's see . . . we met when I was sixteen. My folks had just moved from Portland to Port View. I hated it at first, until I met James—then my world changed. We were in art class together. Most of the boys thought art class was a joke, but not James. He took it seriously and it showed. Everyone loved his work. He even sold a few pieces to teachers. We had our first date right before Thanksgiving—the Harvest Ball. . . ." Grace stared out over the horizon.

"You mean you were sweethearts?" Allison asked in amazement. Grace nodded and Allison was stunned.

"Hey, you lazy beach bums," Winston yelled as he and Heather approached the blanket. "Don't you want to go for a swim with us, Allison?" Just then Andrew and Shirley walked up.

"Sounds like a good plan, little man," Andrew said as he grabbed Winston and threw him over his shoulder. Winston squealed in delight. Allison looked at Grace longingly. She'd happily pass up a swim to hear the rest of this story.

"More later," Grace promised, pushing Allison to her feet.

They gathered their beach bags and trekked to the dressing rooms. Heather and Allison changed quickly and dashed out. Allison glanced down at Marsha's Kelly green swimsuit, the most modest one that Allison could find in Marsha's things. It was a little more sophisticated than she was used to, but at least she liked the color.

"Heather, do you want me to braid your hair so it doesn't get all tangled in the water?" Allison offered. Heather agreed, and they sat in the sand while she carefully braided Heather's long golden curls into one thick braid down her back. "Your hair is so beautiful. In your blue swimsuit, you look just like a mermaid." Heather laughed, and soon the others joined them.

Allison blinked in astonishment when she saw Shirley's bathing suit. It was a metallic-looking thing with gold reptile-like scales. It also appeared Shirley had touched up her makeup. Allison was about to describe Shirley's strange appearance to Heather, but the others were approaching.

"Last one in's a rotten egg!" yelled Winston.

"He sure likes gross things," Allison commented with a laugh. Heather giggled and reached for her hand.

"Allison," she said seriously. "Will you stay with me in the water? I mean, I know how to swim and everything, but I'm a little uncomfortable in the ocean. The waves can throw me for a loop. Andrew usually stays with me, but I don't know where he went. Is he with Shirley again?"

"Where else?" Allison answered. She glanced back at Heather and saw the ocean reflected in her dark green sunglasses. She tried to imagine what it felt like to be blind. Heather seemed so normal, Allison found herself forgetting about her lack of sight. They waded in together, hand in hand. The waves were small and calm in the cove.

"It's freezing! Sure you want to do this?" Allison asked.

"You'll get used to it," reassured Heather. Soon they were swimming and splashing. Together they swam the short way to the end of the large rock that jutted into the bay. Winston and Andrew took turns climbing high and jumping off into the deep end.

"That looks like fun," Allison said.

"Come on up," Andrew called.

"Yeah, unless you're a sissy," Winston teased.

"Go ahead, Allison, I'll be okay," Heather said. Shirley sat nearby on the edge of the rock, her feet in the water.

"Shirley, you keep an eye on Heather," Allison commanded. Allison climbed out and scurried up the rock. Heights usually didn't scare her, but when she got up to the boys she was a bit surprised at how far away the water seemed.

"It's easy," Winston said proudly. "You just plug your nose like this and leap way out." And off he went with a piercing scream.

"It's pretty safe as long as you do it at high tide—like now," Andrew said. Allison looked over the edge with uncertainty.

"What's the matter, Allison, chickening out? Afraid of the water?" Shirley taunted. Shirley, who hadn't even gotten wet yet, had walked out on the rock without swimming.

"Allison, don't jump if you don't want to," Andrew advised. "It's no big deal, you know."

"No—I'm not afraid," Allison replied. She stood on the rock, her toes clinging to the edge, and looked down. The water seemed to get even farther away.

"Heather!" Winston suddenly screamed. "Heather disap-peared beneath the water!"

Without a second thought, Allison leaped from the rock. She plunged down deep into the water and opened her eyes and looked around for Heather. Just as she began to come up, she saw Heather's long golden braid floating under the water just a few feet away. Allison gave a big kick in Heather's direction and grabbed for the braid. Fighting to the surface, she pulled Heather behind her. Both girls came up sputtering out of the water.

"Heather!" Allison gasped. "Are you okay?"

"Yes . . . I think so. Why did you pull me by the hair?"

"I was rescuing you!" Allison exclaimed. By now the others had gathered nearby.

"What happened?" Andrew demanded.

"She just disappeared!" Winston cried. "I was so scared. Heather was gone—I thought she drowned!"

"I lost my sunglasses," Heather explained. "I felt them slip off and down my leg, so I tried to dive for them. I took a deep breath and dove as deep as I could and reached all around, but I couldn't find them. The next thing I knew, someone was tugging me by the hair."

"I'm so sorry, Heather," Allison said. "I thought you were drowning." Heather began to laugh, and before long Allison saw the humor, too.

"Well, you should have seen your face, Allison," Shirley laughed. "It was whiter than a sheet when you jumped. You looked ridiculous!"

Allison glared at her. "Sure, you can laugh. You were supposed to be keeping an eye on Heather! For all you knew, she could have drowned." The words were out of her mouth before she could stop them.

"Come on, Allison," Heather said. "I think I've had enough swimming for now. Besides, I'm freezing."

"Yeah," Andrew agreed. "Hey, it looks like Grace started a bonfire on the beach. Race you, Winston!"

Within minutes they were wrapped up in blankets and towels, huddled around the fire for warmth. Allison made sure to keep a safe distance between her and Shirley. She didn't know how much longer she could control her tongue. Soon the fog started to roll in and the air became cool.

"You kids better go get dressed," Grace advised. "Then we can roast some marshmallows."

After they got into warm clothes, they laughed and joked around the fire. Before long the marshmallows were gone. It appeared that Shirley wasn't about to leave Andrew's side. Allison wondered whether he liked it or not, and to her dismay it almost seemed as if he did. Heather and Grace were chuckling about the "drowning incident," and suddenly Allison felt like the odd man out. She wandered down to the water's edge and picked up a smooth stone, then threw it as far as she could over the curling tops of the waves. Would she ever fit in anywhere?

Twelve

"GRACE, I COULD RIDE in back with the boys," Shirley offered. Her eyes were on Andrew, where he was waiting in the back of the truck with Winston. "That way you three could have more room in front." Heather and Allison listened from inside the jalopy, and Grace looked doubtful.

"Why not?" Andrew suggested. He extended a hand to Shirley and pulled her into the back of the truck, then hopped back out. "You look beat, Grace. Maybe I should drive and give you a rest. Winston, you share that blanket with Shirley, okay? It gets windy back there."

Before Shirley could say anything, Andrew closed the door behind Grace and hopped into the driver's seat. Right next to Allison. He grinned at her and started the engine. At first she felt a little uncomfortable, but then she wished the ride would last forever.

They dropped off a windblown and bedraggled Shirley at her grandmother's, and everyone breathed a sigh of relief. Andrew hopped in back with Winston, and Grace drove from there.

"Grace?" Heather asked. "Could Allison come home with us and spend the night—for my birthday, I mean?"

"Oh, I don't know, Heather. Allison might be tired of us, you know—"

"I'd love to!" Allison exclaimed, but then she remembered her grandfather. "But I'd have to check with Grandpa to see how he's doing. . . ." Allison didn't want to disappoint her. She hoped Grandpa wouldn't mind.

"Would you?" Heather begged. "I've never had anyone spend the night. It could be like a real slumber party. I've read about them but never been to one. It would be such fun! How about if we drop you off and you can check it out with your grandfather." Heather squeezed Allison's hand as they pulled up to the house.

"Okay, then I'll give you a call, Heather." Allison climbed out and waved.

Allison rarely used the front door. It was so much homier to come in through the kitchen, and Muriel didn't seem to mind.

"Home already?" Muriel asked. She carefully slid a loaf of risen bread into the old black oven. "Your grandfather's resting in the den, dear."

"Is he all right?" Allison asked, suddenly filled with dread.

"Oh sure, he's fine. Just tired. He's trying to be good, but sometimes he overdoes it."

Allison tiptoed to the den door and peeked in. Grandpa was stretched out in his easy chair, feet on the hassock and newspaper spread across his lap. The heavy drapes were drawn back, and the afternoon light poured in the bay window.

"Well, lassie, are you going to just stand there gawking or come in and tell me about your picnic?" Grandpa looked at her from the corner of his eye.

Allison laughed and flopped down on the big couch. She leaned her head back and sighed.

"It was an almost perfect day."

"Almost?"

"Yes. Heather is about the nicest girl I've ever known. Grace is wonderful. Winston is hilarious and Andrew is very nice, too."

Grandpa nodded. "You didn't mention Shirley." Allison looked at him and he grinned and winked. "That's all right, you didn't have to." Allison sighed in relief—Grandpa understood.

"Shirley's father, Daniel, is a good man. But he married a very ambitious woman who leads him about by the nose. Poor Dan. Shirley takes after her mother." He smiled at her before continuing.

"Allison, would you tell Muriel I'll take my dinner in here? I'm afraid I fiddled in my workshop a little too long today. Think I'll eat and turn in early. That way we might be able to make it to church in the morning. Haven't been in some time, and I want to show off my granddaughter." He winked.

"Uh, Grandpa, Heather asked if I could spend the night—kind of like a slumber party for her birthday. But I didn't promise her. I can call and make it another time."

"Slumber party?" Grandpa folded his paper and peered at her over his reading glasses.

"Well, yes, that's when girls spend the night together . . . just for fun."

"I don't suppose they do much slumbering, though."

"Not much," Allison laughed. "Would you mind? I can be back in time to join you for church."

"Or you could just meet me there, since Grace and her brood go, too." Grandpa grinned and picked up his paper.

Allison walked to the side of his chair, leaned over, and gave him a kiss on the cheek. He looked up at her and smiled, his eyes glistening. "Thanks, Grandpa. I'll see you in the morning." Allison dashed for the phone.

"I can come, Heather!" She held the receiver away from her ear while Heather squealed, then raced upstairs and threw some overnight things in her bag. *Oh yes—church*, she thought. She folded the peach rayon suit and wished she had something more appropriate for a fourteen-year-old. She was getting tired of Marsha's clothes.

Downstairs the smell of baked bread filled the kitchen, and Allison's mouth watered.

"Muriel, maybe it's too bad Heather invited me for dinner. It smells awfully yummy in here."

"Well, Heather's a sweet little thing, and I think it's nice you get to spend some time with her. If you wait a few minutes, one

of these loaves should be ready and you could take it to Grace
for a hostess gift."

"Good thinking, Muriel. That's the best kind of hostess gift.
It's like having your cake and eating it, too."

Muriel chuckled. "Do you need George to drive you over?
He's been to town running errands, but he should be back any
minute."

"No, that's okay. Andrew's picking me up." She glanced out
the window at the driveway.

"That Andrew . . . he's awfully nice." Muriel gave Allison a
sideways glance and Allison blushed. "I'd say Grace was as
lucky as those kids when they found one another." She wrapped
the bread in a heavy linen tea towel and handed it to Allison.

"There he is, Muriel. Thanks for the bread. See you tomorrow." Allison zipped out the door, and Andrew put her bag in
the back of the truck.

As they drove out, Allison noticed George carrying a large
wooden box up the driveway. "That's odd," she commented.

"What's that?" Andrew asked.

"Oh, nothing really. Just Muriel said George was in town
running errands, but I wouldn't think he would've walked." Allison remembered the list in the shed.

"No, I doubt it. I just saw him coming up from the dock as
I drove in. He's probably been out fishing or something."

"Oh sure," Allison said. "I didn't know George liked to fish.
Maybe I can get him to take me out in the rowboat sometime.
Grandpa didn't seem to want me to go out alone, although I do
know how to handle a boat in the tide. I spent most of my summers on Cape Cod."

"Really? I'd love to learn more about boats and fishing, but
I've never gotten around to it. How long do you plan on visiting
your grandfather, Allison? Maybe you could give me a lesson or
two."

"That's a good question. I'm not really sure how long I'll be able to stay." She decided to confide in Andrew and filled him in on some of the details of her escape.

"Are you serious? You actually traveled by yourself all the way from New York without your mother's permission?" He shook his head in amazement.

"Well, under the circumstances, I just did what I had to do." Allison gave him a sidelong glance as they pulled into the driveway. What did he think of her now? She wanted to continue their conversation, but she was interrupted by Heather's greeting.

"Come in, come in. Grace said dinner's almost ready. Andrew, will you put her things in my room?"

"Certainly, Your Highness." He bowed and winked at Allison.

"Thank you so much. You may kiss the royal hand later," Heather laughed.

Allison marveled at how effortlessly Heather made her way through the house. First she showed Allison the living room. It looked so cozy with overstuffed furniture in bright floral slipcovers all clustered around the fireplace. Above the fireplace hung a large, dark oil painting. It seemed such a contrast to the colorful surroundings, and yet it captivated Allison with its intensity and what almost seemed like rage. It depicted a small white lighthouse with a steady beam that sliced through the darkness of a wild and violent storm. It looked a lot like the Jenson Light, although she'd never seen the lighthouse close enough to know for sure.

"Dinner's ready," Grace announced, breaking the hypnotic trance the painting seemed to hold on her.

"I almost forgot," Allison turned away. "Muriel sent over some fresh-baked bread." She handed the warm bundle to Grace.

"Mmm, smells good," Winston said, licking his lips.

They sat at the big oak dining table and bowed their heads

to pray. Allison was getting used to this tradition. It was nothing like Miss Snyder's cold, formal prayers back at Oakmont. It reminded her more of how Nanny Jane used to talk to God, and it gave her a warm, peaceful feeling inside.

"Pass the potatoes, Mum," Winston said almost as soon as Grace finished.

"Say please," Grace corrected with a smile.

"Delicious roast, Grace," Andrew commented. Allison nodded in agreement.

After the meal, Grace brought out a pretty pink cake with fourteen candles burning brightly. They all sang loudly, and Winston assisted in the candle blowing.

"Do you know what color it is?" Winston asked.

"Pink!" Heather exclaimed.

"How did you know?" Allison asked in amazement. "Was it the smell or something?"

"No," Heather giggled. "Grace already told me, silly!" They all laughed.

Afterward Winston listened to the *Green Hornet* on the big radio in the living room while Andrew helped Grace with the dishes. The girls slipped off into Heather's bedroom to visit. Heather had a phonograph and a pretty good collection of seventy-eights. They listened to Bing Crosby and Glenn Miller and then some more lively tunes.

"You know, Allison, I know it's kind of old-fashioned now, but I always wished I could learn to jitterbug."

"Really? Maybe I could teach you."

"You're joking! Do you really know how? Teach me!"

"I can try. My friend Patricia at school was really good at it— her big sister even won a dance contest once. And Patricia taught me. Let's see . . ." Allison searched her brain for ideas on how to teach Heather. First she tried to explain the steps, but it was just too complicated.

"Maybe we should just try it," Heather suggested. So they

picked out a good record, then stumbled and fumbled and collapsed in giggles occasionally. Finally Heather caught on.

"Heather, you're doing swell!"

"Once you get the hang of it, it's really fun. But do I look ridiculous?"

"No, you don't. To be honest, you looked a little goofy at first, but that's just normal. Now you're almost perfect." A knock at the door interrupted their dance number.

"What's going on in here?" Andrew asked. "Sounds like a herd of elephants doing the cha-cha."

"Allison's teaching me how to jitterbug!"

"You're joking," Andrew said. Grace and Winston peeked in behind him.

"No, it's true!" Heather's cheeks were flushed with excitement. "Look, we'll even show you!"

"Uh, I don't know. . . ." Allison suddenly became self-conscious at the idea of performing, especially in front of Andrew.

"Oh please, Al," Heather begged, pulling Allison out to the living room. Andrew quickly rolled up the carpet and scooted the furniture back.

"Now, nobody better laugh," Allison threatened. Grace started the music and the girls began. Heather only stepped on Allison's toe once. After a few quick lessons, they were all jitterbugging. The next thing Allison knew, Andrew had taken her by the hand.

Winston, who was jittering like a broken washing machine, suddenly spun himself right into the phonograph and jolted the needle across the record in a loud, angry scratch.

"I'm sorry, Heather," Winston apologized as the record played the same line over and over.

"It's all right, Winston," Heather said. "I didn't really like that song very much. Besides, I'm exhausted. Where's a couch?"

"And bedtime for you, Winston," Grace announced.

"Aw, Mum, can't I stay up? It's just getting fun!"

"No, but if you hurry and get your jammies on, I'll read you some more of *Robin Hood*," Andrew offered, and Winston was off just like an arrow out of his hero's bow. Grace and Allison soon set the living room right while Heather rattled some pots and pans in the kitchen.

"Heather's so amazing," Allison commented. "She even knows how to help in the kitchen?"

"You bet. We have everything arranged so she can easily find things. Andrew even typed spice labels on the Braille typewriter. I think the best thing for Heather is to live as normal a life as possible. In other words, we don't baby her." Grace fluffed a pillow and tossed it to the sofa.

"Grace, you know—about my dad. I was just wondering if you could tell me a bit more, maybe tonight. . . ."

"Grace," Heather called. "Can you give me a hand in here?"

"We'll talk later," Grace promised. "Let's go see what Heather's getting into."

In the pint-sized kitchen, Heather already had cocoa steaming on the range.

"Smells good," Grace said. "Want me to pour?"

"Thanks," Heather replied. "Actually, I was wondering about some popcorn."

"Hey, sounds like a swell idea," Andrew said, appearing in the doorway. "Why don't you ladies take your cocoa into the living room, and let me show you how a man can take care of himself in the kitchen."

Grace lit the fire in the fireplace, and the three sipped cocoa and visited happily like old friends.

"Allison, do you want me to tell you more now?" Grace asked, nodding toward Heather questioningly.

"Oh sure, I wish you would. Heather, I asked Grace to tell me more about my dad. She's the only one who seems willing to talk about him. You don't mind, do you?"

"No. In fact, I was rather curious myself."

"Well, let me see . . ." began Grace. "I already told you how we met in high school."

"Yes, Heather, they were sweethearts—can you believe it? Grace and my father!"

Heather shook her head in obvious amazement.

Allison studied Grace; the way her hair shone in the firelight and the warmth of her deep brown eyes. She could imagine her father falling in love with Grace, perhaps even more easily than with Marsha. Andrew entered with the popcorn but said nothing. He sat silently on the floor by the fire and placed the gigantic bowl on the low coffee table. Grace looked at Allison again, as if to ask whether to continue or not. Allison nodded.

"Well, it's true we were sweethearts. James was a year older than I, but we continued to date even after he graduated. He worked with his father in the shipping business that year, but it was 1929—not a good year for business. Only a few years earlier, Riley had incorporated the shipping business and sold stocks in order to build the lighthouse."

Allison nodded. She remembered that part of Grandpa's story.

"Anyway," Grace continued, "that fall when the market crashed, Riley's stockholders—mostly locals—were furious. They wanted refunds on their stock. Riley did what he could for them and nearly sunk his shipping business in the process."

"You mean he sold their stocks back to them?" Andrew asked incredulously. "No one else would have done that."

"And it made it very hard on the O'Brians. He and James bitterly disagreed over it, and that's when James decided to strike out on his own. He had always loved to paint, so he decided to go to New York and try to make something of his art. Our high school art teacher had told him about Greenwich Village, and it had been James' dream to go there and live among the artists. I guess the problems with the business gave him the excuse he needed to leave Oregon."

"But what about you?" Heather asked sympathetically.

"Well, I didn't like the idea of James leaving. We even had a fight about it. It's not that I didn't want him to pursue his dream. It's just that I felt Riley needed him right then more than ever. But stubborn old Riley wouldn't admit it or ask James to stay. Mercury was brokenhearted, but she gave James her blessing and a bit of money to start him out." Allison followed Grace's gaze up to the dark painting above the fireplace. Grace's eyes looked misty.

"Did he paint it?" Allison's voice was no more than a whisper. Grace nodded. They all stared at the painting in silence.

"What happened then?" Heather asked.

"Well, at first James and I wrote regularly, but after my first year of nursing school in Portland, we lost touch. I wrote several times without hearing back. Finally I decided not to write again until I heard from him. . . ." Her voice choked with emotion. "The next thing I knew he was married." Grace stared into the fire, and Allison wished there were something she could say. She felt almost sorry she'd encouraged Grace to talk about it. She'd had no idea. . . .

"Well, Grace," Andrew stated, "James must've been a bit of a fool. Sorry, Allison."

"To be truthful, Andrew, I'd have to agree with you. You see, the woman he married, my mother, isn't half as nice as Grace." Andrew and Heather looked surprised.

"Of course, if he hadn't married Marsha, I guess I wouldn't be here. . . ."

"Life certainly has some unexplainable twists in it," Grace said.

"What you told me tonight helps to fill in some gaps, but there is still so much more." Allison stared at the painting as if searching for a clue.

"I can tell you what I heard after that, though I can't guarantee it's all true. Mercury and I continued to keep in touch while I was in nursing school. I was lucky to have something to throw myself into. Mercury told me that James gave up his art when a baby came along. That would've been you. It seemed that Marsha's parents had connections that helped him land a job in insurance. Then Marsha's career began to take off, and after that the war came. I joined the Red Cross, and the next thing I heard about James was that he'd been killed—" Her voice choked.

The fire crackled and Allison felt a lump grow in her throat. She swallowed and attempted to speak. "Grace, did you ever hear about a scandal with my dad in the insurance company?"

Grace smoothed her hand over a cushion. "Yes, I remember Mercury telling me—it was summer of '42, I believe, and the last time I ever saw her. I stopped by to tell them good-bye just before I left on assignment for England. She mentioned you, Allison, and how she'd been getting your room ready for your visit. And then about the awful letter she'd gotten. Accusing James of embezzlement, I think it was. She didn't believe a word of it, though. She suspected it was some sort of scam to get him out of Marsha's life. I didn't believe it, either. James might've been a bit foolish, but he wasn't a thief."

Allison shook her head sadly, hoping Grace was right. It was bad enough having Marsha as a mother, but she couldn't bear to think her father had been a crook. Just then she remembered the letter from Marsha's closet safe.

"You know, Grace, I discovered this old letter at Marsha's—" She didn't want to go into the details of how she'd been snooping. "It seemed as if it had been written to clear my dad's name. I brought it with me, though I don't know exactly why."

"Really? Well, you should definitely share it with Riley. Even though James is gone, I don't think Riley's ever forgiven him. You never know, the letter might help him. Unforgiveness is a horrible thing. It can eat away a person's soul. . . ."

There was a long silence. Allison stared up at the painting.

It was so intense. So full of pain. She thought about the note in the garden shed, and the letter *J*. "I have this really weird feeling. . . ." she began.

"What is it?" Grace asked. Heather and Andrew leaned forward to listen. The fire crackled loudly, and Allison's eyes were pulled up to the painting again.

"It sounds so incredibly foolish. I don't even want to say it out loud. You'll think I'm crazy."

"Go ahead, Allison, we're your friends," Andrew said.

"Well, I just keep getting this feeling that my dad is alive." She heard Grace gasp. She knew it was ridiculous. What was wrong with her, anyway?

"Oh, Allison," Grace whispered. "I don't know what to say. I know how much you must wish he were alive. . . ."

"That's not it, Grace. Not completely. I just . . . well . . . I keep getting this feeling."

Heather reached over and placed her hand on Allison's arm. "I know what you mean, Allison. Sometimes I feel like my mum is still alive. I think I can hear her singing when I'm on the beach. But I think it's just God's way of comforting me, you know? Reminding me that she's okay and I'll see her again."

Allison nodded, but it *wasn't* the same. The feeling she had about her dad wasn't comforting. It was disturbing and haunting. Like a demanding question that kept rattling around in her head.

Thirteen

THE NEXT MORNING ALLISON awoke early. Heather still slept soundly, but Allison had hardly slept at all. She couldn't stop thinking about her dad. Was it because of the things that Grace had shared, or was there something else? Maybe he was just becoming more real since she was finally getting to know a little bit about him. Even though she was tired, she knew she couldn't stay in bed another minute. She quietly dressed and slipped down to the beach.

The sun was barely up and the sky was a soft periwinkle blue. A gentle breeze tickled the air. She sat on a rock and watched the waves tumble in, one after another. Her mind was partly numb by the thoughts that had haunted her all night. What if her dad had never met Marsha Madison? Would he have married Grace? Would he still be alive? Was there any chance that he might still be alive? She had heard stories of people getting identities confused in the war. Maybe that could—no, she had to stop thinking like this! Everyone knew her dad was dead.

She stared out into the sea. A glassy blue peak rose straight from the water, smooth and sleek, as if chiseled from stone. Then just as quickly it curled and was swallowed by foamy white surf.

Suddenly, she wished she were with Grandpa, sitting at the big mahogany table overlooking the garden and eating breakfast across from him. What if something was wrong? What if he'd had heart problems again last night? He'd looked so tired yesterday. Maybe she should run back and—

"Hey, down there," Winston called from on top of the bluff.

"If ya wanna eat breakfast, you better hurry up!" She waved and tried to dismiss her troublesome thoughts. She knew she was letting her imagination get the best of her. She scampered up the steps, reminding herself she would soon see Grandpa at church.

Inside, Andrew handed her a plate of hotcakes and sausage. The others were just sitting down.

"Sorry . . . I lost track of the time. It's so pretty down there." Allison looked around. "And you're all ready for church."

"Oh, don't worry," Heather replied. "The service doesn't start for a couple hours."

Allison helped Grace in the kitchen, then hurried off to change for church.

"What are you wearing?" Heather asked as she slowly pulled a satin ribbon back and forth between her fingers. Allison was once again reminded of her friend's visual handicap.

"You know, Heather, I keep forgetting you can't see—with your eyes, I mean. It seems you see so much without them. I'm wearing a summer suit that's really Marsha's . . . I mean my mother's. It's a peachy kind of color, like pink. But it really looks too old for me. My normal clothes got sent to that stupid old summer camp. Remember I told you all about it—Camp Horrible." Heather laughed as they walked outside to meet the others.

"Wow, you look all grown up, Allison," Winston commented.

"Lovely suit," said Grace. Allison's face burned in embarrassment when she realized she was wearing the clothes of the same woman who'd stolen Grace's beau.

It was a quiet ride. Allison watched the landscape roll by through the salt-streaked jalopy windows. They pulled up to an old church building made entirely of stone. High stained-glass windows sparkled in the sun, and a stone steeple bore an old, weathered cross. Allison instantly spotted Grandpa standing with Muriel and George in the gravel parking lot.

"If you don't mind, I'll join Grandpa now. Thanks so very much for everything." She looked at Grace, then squeezed Heather's hand. "I'll see you later." She jumped down and called to Grandpa.

Inside the church, the windows glowed in rich jewel tones. It was a small building, but something about the thick stone walls and heavy oak furniture gave an atmosphere of grandeur that could compete with any East Coast church.

In front of Allison and Grandpa sat Beatrice Jenson with Shirley. Shirley wore a bright pink suit with a matching wide-brimmed hat that managed to entirely block Allison's view of the pulpit. Allison tilted her head to and fro, but it was hopeless. She'd have to just imagine what the preacher looked like. The pink feather on Shirley's hat kept turning slightly to the left time and again. Allison peered over to see what interested Miss Jenson so. Andrew sat in the opposite aisle, his eyes focused on the pulpit. It figured.

Before long, the little choir in the loft sang their final song, and Allison realized the service was over. She could hardly remember what had been said, but she thought it was something about forgiveness. Hadn't Grace said something about how unforgiveness could eat a person's soul? Maybe Allison should've listened better.

"Good sermon, Reverend Simmons." Riley shook the preacher's hand. "This is my granddaughter, Allison O'Brian."

She shook his hand and studied his face. It was the first real look she'd gotten, and he wasn't nearly as old as she'd imagined. In fact, he had a very nice smile.

"James' daughter? Why, your father was a very good friend of mine. It's a great pleasure to meet you, Allison O'Brian." He patted her on the back, then looked over her shoulder with a bright smile. Allison glanced back to see Grace coming down the steps behind her.

"Good morning, Grace." Reverend Simmons' face was all lit

up. "And how are you on this fine, sunny day?" It seemed he held Grace's hand just a little longer than necessary, and Allison winked at Grace as she continued down the steps.

"I thought we'd drive down to Port View for lunch," Grandpa suggested. "Give Muriel the afternoon off. What do you say, George?" Grandpa and Allison climbed into the spacious backseat of the car.

"Sounds like a good plan," George agreed. Muriel nodded her consent as George closed her door. Allison loved the way Grandpa treated George and Muriel more like family than employees. She remembered how Grandmother Madison had always treated Nanny Jane like a slave. It still irritated her to think of it.

"Did you have a good nightgown party?"

"You mean pajama party," Allison corrected. "Yes, it was terrific. And Grace is wonderful. It was fun getting to know her. I wonder if she'll ever marry again. Is Reverend Simmons married? He seemed to be making sheep's eyes at her." Muriel chuckled in the front seat and George grunted.

"As a matter of fact, he's not married," Grandpa answered. "Never gave it much thought, but now that you mention it, he does seem awfully fond of her." He scratched his head thoughtfully, but his face looked slightly troubled.

Before long, a sign announced they were entering Port View. Grandpa pointed out a big brick building. "That's Port View High School, where Heather will go next fall. Of course, Andrew's already there."

Allison wished with all her heart that she could go, too. Maybe something would work out by the end of summer. Maybe Marsha would let Allison stay with Grandpa. Her thoughts were cut off when George parked in front of a plain white stucco building with big blue letters—Molly's Chowder House.

"Doesn't look like much, but they've got the best seafood

you've ever eaten," Grandpa commented as he held the door for Allison. The tables were covered in blue gingham oilcloth, and a bank of windows allowed patrons to view the fishing boats docked down on the wharf. They sat at a table by a window, and Allison peered down to a fishing rig below. A grizzled fisherman sorted out his nets while another busily gutted fish, throwing the scraps into a bloody bucket.

"Ugh, that'll sure ruin your appetite," Allison said. They all looked down and laughed.

"Yep, cutting bait. I used to do that all the time," Grandpa mused. He launched into an exciting fishing story that lasted most of the meal.

Allison finished her last giant prawn and groaned. "I'm stuffed. You're right about this place, Grandpa. It even beats my favorite chowder house on the Cape."

"Is that a fact? Well, we O'Brians know our seafood." He placed his last empty crab leg onto a big pile of shells.

Feeling the need to work off their enormous lunch, they slowly strolled down the waterfront street. Most of the shops were closed, but they bought some saltwater taffy at the candy store and went down to the docks. Grandpa admired a couple of commercial fishing boats, pointing out some new modern features. Soon the fog rolled in and the breeze picked up, and they all hurried back to the car.

On the ride home Grandpa looked tired. Allison was worried about his health—and her own future. What would become of her without him? He seemed her last shred of hope for any kind of normal life. She wished she could stay with him forever. She remembered the letter she'd written to Marsha . . . if only Muriel hadn't mailed it. Then Marsha wouldn't know. And how long would it be before Marsha responded? Allison shook her head, hoping to toss off those disturbing thoughts.

"Say, George, do you ever go fishing?" she asked, looking for some conversation to distract her from her worries.

Muriel laughed. "Not hardly, dear. George can barely stand the sight of a boat without getting queasy. Your grandfather took him out once years ago and brought him back pea green."

George sniffed indignantly. "Well, it was pretty rough out that day." He guided the car down the driveway and past the dock road.

Allison recalled how she'd seen him there last night. Andrew had felt fairly certain that George had been out on the boat. But why would George deny it? And why was he carrying that big empty box?

Grandpa retired to the den to rest, and Allison went up to her room to change. As usual, the sunny room welcomed her like an old friend. She put away her things and tried to settle down with *Gone With the Wind* again. It was hard to concentrate, but finally the story took her mind off other nagging thoughts. Before she knew it she'd drifted to sleep and awoke to Muriel's gentle nudging.

"Sorry to wake you, dear, but supper's ready and I thought you might get hungry."

Allison rubbed her eyes. "Yes, of course. Thanks, Muriel, I'll be down in a jiff."

The table in the dining room was set for just her and Grandpa. Tonight there were only two candles burning, but the roses were still there. The blooms were fully opened and had faded to a soft, pale pink. A few limp petals lay on the polished table.

"Just a light supper tonight," Muriel announced as she ladled a clear amber soup into Allison's bowl.

"That's fine. I'm still pretty full from lunch." She sipped the steaming broth. "Delicious, Muriel." Grandpa seemed quieter than usual. "Are you feeling okay, Grandpa?" She studied his face for clues.

"Well, I'm feeling a wee bit tired tonight, lassie. I think I'll have my soup and then put my feet up in the den again."

Allison finished her soup and poked at her salad. Even Muriel's fresh-baked bread didn't interest her tonight. She cleared the table, then checked on Grandpa in the den. He reclined in his big chair with his feet on the hassock, his eyes closed. She tiptoed closer, wanting to make sure he was still breathing. His chest rose and fell rhythmically, and she draped an afghan gently over his legs. Slipping back out, she joined Muriel in the kitchen to help dry dishes.

"I'm worried about Grandpa, Muriel." Allison placed a teacup in the china cabinet. "He seems a bit off tonight. Did you notice?"

"Well, not particularly. . . . You know, tomorrow's Monday and generally our day off. We were planning a trip to Portland, but if you think it's necessary, we can stick around—"

"Oh no. You go enjoy your day off. I'll be here with Grandpa. I'm probably just making a mountain of a molehill. I just get so worried when I think about his health."

"The doctor said when he goes he goes, and no one can do anything about it one way or another." Muriel said the words matter-of-factly, but Allison heard the catch in her voice.

"I'm sure that's true. It's just I don't know if I could take it." Allison twisted the dish towel in her hands and stared at the floor.

Muriel wrapped her arms around Allison. "Don't you worry, darling. He's such a strong-willed ol' codger."

"Thanks. I think I'll go and sit with him awhile." She quietly slipped into the chair by the fireplace. There was no fire burning tonight. She stared into the black grate. Empty and cold. Just how her heart would feel if she lost Grandpa. She knew how it felt to lose her father and Nanny Jane, and even Grandmother Mercury, whom she'd never known. She was certain she couldn't handle losing anyone else.

"Hey, Allison, what're you doing sitting there in the dark?"

Grandpa sat up in his chair with a big grin. "Turn on the light, lassie."

She rose to turn on the lights but stopped first to admire the rosy sunset outside. "Isn't that beautiful, Grandpa? Is it really true what they say? Red sky at night, sailors delight. Red sky at morning, sailors take warning."

"Some swear by it, but most good fishermen will tell you it's no guarantee." She watched the sky grow into an even darker and more intense shade of red. Maybe it was a signal that everything was okay for her and Grandpa.

"Grandpa, Grace told me a bit about my father." She sat on the ottoman in front of him. Once again, Grandpa's face clouded, and Allison knew he didn't want to speak of his son. "And there's something I need to show you." She picked her words carefully and deliberately. "I hope it will help you to see my father in a whole new light. You wait here and I'll be right back."

She dashed up the stairs. It seemed to take forever to find the letter. She hadn't planned to break it to him like this, but something inside compelled her. She had a new sense of urgency. This couldn't wait! Maybe it had to do with forgiveness. She vaguely remembered Reverend Simmons' words on forgiveness, along with what Grace had said about how unforgiveness could eat your soul. Those were strong words! But maybe—maybe if Grandpa could forgive her dad—maybe that would help him to get well, or at least heal his broken heart. She flew down the stairs and into the den.

"I brought this letter and almost forgot about it. You see, I found it in Marsha's things," she explained breathlessly, thrusting the envelope at him. He lifted a brow in suspicion. "Well, the truth is I was snooping. Grandpa, no one would tell me anything . . . and my life is so full of unanswered questions. I just had to take the bull by the horns, so to speak. . . ."

Grandpa grinned and opened the envelope.

She waited impatiently for him to adjust his reading glasses. At last he removed the letter and carefully unfolded it. She studied his face for any expression as he read, but it was as blank as the back of the letter.

"Hmm." He slowly refolded the letter and replaced it in the envelope, then shook his head as if trying to understand its meaning. His face bore a puzzled expression. Allison wasn't sure if it was good or bad. Then he removed the letter again. She watched his eyes moving quickly this time, and his hands began to tremble. He scanned the envelope, studying the postmark, and turned it over and over in his hands.

"Do you remember how old you were when Marsha told you about your father's death?" he asked.

"Eight, almost nine. Why?"

"Oh, I just wondered if Marsha had received this letter before it was too late. I wonder if she made any effort to get this news to him. . . ." His voice sounded thick and he looked away. A tear glistened on his weathered cheek, and she went over to try to comfort him but instead burst into tears.

"Oh, Grandpa, I love you so much, and it hurts me to see how you've felt about my father all these years. I'm sorry, but I just had to say it." Now Grandpa cried quietly, and the sound of his sobs turned her heart inside out. She wished desperately to take back her words.

"Grandpa, I'm so thankful I have you. I need you so much—"

A knock interrupted Allison; Muriel stood in the doorway. Her eyes were wide and her face was white. Her eyes locked with Allison as she addressed Grandpa. "It's a telegram, Mr. O'Brian. I'm terribly sorry to interrupt, but it's from New York and I fear it may be urgent."

At the sound of the words "New York," Allison's sadness turned to fear. What could this mean? Had Marsha already received her letter?

Muriel handed the telegram to Grandpa. "I'll make some tea, Mr. O'Brian."

He took a deep breath and blew his nose. Allison sat frozen to her chair, watching breathlessly. Leave it to Marsha to have such perfectly horrible timing!

"Whatever this is, we can take it. We're O'Brians, after all." He opened the bright yellow envelope. For a second Allison hoped it was news of an airplane wreck involving Marsha. Then she shamefully retracted the awful thought.

He cleared his throat and read. " 'Mr. O'Brian stop—Marsha has wired from Istanbul stop—Allison to return immediately stop—Secretary Lola Stevens will travel to pick up Allison stop—We expect your full cooperation stop—Anthony Meyer, Attorney at Law stop.' "

Grandpa leaned back and closed his eyes as silence filled the room. Allison sunk deep into a chair like a deflated balloon. Muriel entered and set the tea tray on the table before them. Mutely she poured, but her shaking hand rattled the teacup against the saucer, interrupting the otherwise quiet room.

"I suppose you heard, Muriel." Grandpa spoke calmly, and Muriel nodded. "Well, send George in. I need him to run an important errand for me."

"Oh, I'm so sorry, sir. You see, George and I were going over to Portland tomorrow to visit his nephew, and I just sent him on ahead without me. I felt I might be needed here. Of course, this was before the telegram. Anything I can do, sir?"

"No, no thanks, Muriel. I'll figure something out."

Allison nervously sipped her tea and watched Grandpa. His face was a study of emotions now. She could see he was thinking very hard, and it reminded her of when he played chess. But what was he going to do?

"Grandpa, I'm so sorry. I should have told you about how I came, but I didn't want to upset you. You've probably already guessed . . . I came on my own—without Marsha's permission.

It's a long story, but I had to see you. And they were just going to ship me off to some horrible summer camp. I didn't think anyone would care that I left. But I'm sorry I lied. I didn't know what else to do."

"Don't worry, lassie. And while I don't care much for lying, I'm not the least bit mad at you. I suspected something like this all along. I never really thought that Marsha had let you come. I'm thankful you did what you did, but I wish you could have come with your mother's permission. It wasn't right to deceive her. Now, if we could just figure a way to keep you here. That is, if you want to stay—"

"More than anything, Grandpa! My greatest wish is that I could stay here with you forever! This feels like a real home to me."

"That's my wish, too, lassie. First of all I need to write my lawyer and have him examine the legal implications of this letter. It's a very good thing you brought it, Allison. It's helped me in more ways than you know, but we'll talk more about that later. Right now I've a lot to do. You two better clear on out for a bit."

For once it almost seemed like Allison's gray cloud was gone. Surely Grandpa could fix anything!

Fourteen

ALLISON TRIED NOT TO DISTURB Grandpa as he worked at his desk, surrounded by papers. It was late, but she still heard him pecking on his big black typewriter. He'd find a way to keep her here!

"Care to join me for some cocoa?"

Allison looked up to see Muriel standing in the doorway. She mechanically followed her to the kitchen, her thoughts tumbling around in her head. What if she were seeing everything in this wonderful old house for the last time? What if Lola came with the police and snatched her away? In a daze she studied the orderly kitchen. She wanted to imprint her memory with each copper pot, the old wood stove, even Muriel in her worn chenille bathrobe.

"Allison," Muriel began as she poured steamy milk into a blue and white cup, "if anyone can figure a way out of this, it's your grandfather. He's been through so much in his life, and somehow he always comes out on top."

Allison smiled. "The unsinkable Riley O'Brian."

"I guess that about sums it up."

"Well, I hope you're right." They sat in companionable silence while Allison finished her cocoa. She tried desperately to stay awake, but her eyelids were too heavy to keep open.

"You need some rest. Time for bed, darling." Muriel rinsed the cups in the deep sink.

"What about Grandpa? He needs his rest, too."

"I learned long ago you can lead a horse to water, but you cannot make him drink. And that grandfather of yours can be as stubborn as a mule. He'll go to bed when he's good and ready." She turned off the kitchen lights and headed to her quarters behind the house.

Grandpa was still busy at his desk, so Allison wandered into the parlor. Even though she was tired, she felt too restless for sleep. Instead she switched on an elegant lamp with an intricate rose painted on its base. She hadn't spent much time in this room, and Grandpa seemed to avoid it. She curled up in a corner of the soft velvety couch and studied the pretty decor. She could definitely see Grandmother Mercury's touch in the delicate furnishings and soft pastel colors. A large green palm in a big pot thrived by the window. Allison wondered if Grandmother Mercury had spent a lot of time in here—perhaps on this very couch admiring the same plant.

She closed her eyes and imagined her grandmother's skirts swishing through the house. She tried to picture her father as a young boy. It was difficult since she couldn't even remember ever seeing him. The most she could conjure up was a faceless child with bright red hair.

Soon her imaginings turned into strange dreams. A woman in a swishing skirt wandered aimlessly through the vacant house. She was wringing her hands and moaning for her lost Jamie. But suddenly the woman changed into Marsha, and the faceless child with red hair ran wailing up the stairs. The stairs stretched on and on, and the faceless child became Allison. At last she reached the top and looked over her shoulder. Marsha was stealing up from behind, and the floor before Allison dropped away into a giant abyss.

She awoke trembling and in a cold sweat, but the pretty lamp still glowed with a friendly light. She sighed and realized she was still safe in Grandpa's house. Creeping down the darkened hallway, she found the den dark and empty. At least Grandpa had finally gone to bed. She tiptoed up the stairs and past his bedroom door. It was slightly ajar, and, as usual, she peeked in to reassure herself all was well. Grandpa's bed was still made and unslept in.

With concern, she opened the door wide and looked around. Where was he? She flicked on the light and looked at the little nautical clock above his fireplace. *Two* A.M.*!* What in the world could he be doing at this time of night? His bathroom door was open and unoccupied. She went back downstairs again. Still all the lights were off and no traces of Grandpa. Should she awaken Muriel, or was there some logical explanation?

She decided to check the garage. The cars were all there except for George's little Ford, but she knew he'd have taken it to Portland. She walked through the garden and past the darkened shed, then peered into Grandpa's workshop. No sign of him. She wandered down the driveway aimlessly, looking to the left and right. She searched for some clue, some trace, anything. . . . He couldn't just disappear.

Finally she reached the dock road. It was black as ink, but a ray from the Jenson Light passed through the trees and gave her enough courage to continue. It was as if the light was drawing her toward the water. Halfway down the road she told herself she was crazy. She was about to turn back when she noticed something rocking in the water just a short distance from the dock. It looked like a boat. How odd to have a boat out in the middle of the night.

She ran down to the dock for a better look, but it was so dark she could barely make it out. It appeared to be the rowboat. Just then the beam from the lighthouse moved slowly across the small boat and illuminated a slumped-over form inside. She instantly recognized Grandpa's plaid lumber jacket and screamed. The figure moved ever so slightly.

She kicked off her shoes and plunged into the water. The coldness shocked her and her clothes encased and tugged on her, but she swam hard. The distance between her and the boat seemed to be expanding. The tide was going out! She couldn't make herself turn back—she had to reach the boat. She fought not only for Grandpa's life now but also for her own.

At last she hauled her exhausted, soggy body into the boat, dripping, shaking, and numb with cold. She checked Grandpa—he was still breathing. She gently laid him back against the bow of the boat.

"Please be okay, Grandpa," she breathed. "I'll get you to shore. Just hang on. Please hang on!" She eased the oars from his grasp, then began to row with all her might against the tide. At first she was so stiff from cold that she felt clumsy and un-coordinated, but before long she settled into a rhythm that was almost like a prayer. *Just make it to shore. Just make it to shore.* It felt like an eternity, but finally she reached the dock, leaped out, and tied the boat securely.

"Hang on, Grandpa! I'm going to get help." She ran up the dock and raced straight for Muriel's quarters. She screamed and pounded on the door until Muriel opened up with a ghostly white face.

"Call Dr. Hartley," Allison gasped. "It's Grandpa! Down at the dock! Get Grace and Andrew over—we need help!" Without explaining, she ripped the blankets off Muriel's bed and raced back for the dock. Her mind sped faster than her feet. *Is he still alive? Will he be okay?*

"I'm coming, Grandpa!" she screamed in a voice hoarse from fear and exhaustion. When she finally reached the boat, Grandpa was still breathing, but his face appeared to be in pain. She wrapped one blanket around him and tucked the other un-der his head for a pillow. When would somebody get there?

She held his cold hand in hers and prayed a silent, desperate prayer. A prayer without words that only her heart could com-prehend. His hand squeezed hers ever so slightly.

"Please don't die, Grandpa," she whispered. "Please don't die. I love you so much. I need you." Hot tears began to slide down her cheeks. Muriel came running down the road, her bathrobe fluttering. Behind her came a set of headlights bouncing on the dock road.

Grace and Andrew leaped out of the jalopy. Together the four of them eased Grandpa out of the boat and onto a thick quilt that Andrew had spread out on the ground. They used it as a lift to carry him and gently laid him in the back of the flatbed. Andrew drove for the house while Grace cared for Grandpa in back.

"That was smart to think of calling Grace," Muriel said with her arm around Allison. "Next best thing to the doctor and quicker. Doc Hartley should be here soon, though." They all got Grandpa into the den and laid him on the couch.

"Is he still on digitalis?" Grace asked.

"Yes, he keeps it in his pocket." Muriel removed the vial and handed it to Grace. "What if he already took some?"

"More won't hurt," Grace said. She slipped two into his mouth and held it closed. "Come on, Riley, hold on. Hold on for Allison." She glanced at Allison. "You get out of those wet things right now!"

Allison didn't move. "I have to stay with Grandpa."

"Muriel, take her," Grace commanded.

"Come on, darling." Muriel led Allison by the arm. "It won't do him any good to have you catch pneumonia." Muriel looked down at her bathrobe. "I better get dressed, too. Grace will handle things for now."

"Here comes Dr. Hartley," Andrew called from the front door.

Allison dashed to her room and peeled off her soggy clothes. Her skin looked strangely white in the mirror as she ripped her dry clothes over her still-damp skin. She bolted back downstairs just as Dr. Hartley, Andrew, and Grace carried Grandpa out to the doctor's car.

"We haven't time for the ambulance," Grace explained. "Riley needs to get to the hospital in Port View now. Allison, you come with me. Andrew will bring Muriel."

Grace sat in back and tended to Grandpa, and Allison rode in front with the doctor. She'd never seen anyone drive so fast, but she was sure he knew every curve in the road. She wished he could drive even faster. After what seemed like forever, they pulled up to a large brick building. Three men in white uniforms zipped out with a stretcher bed and expertly loaded Grandpa. With Dr. Hartley on their heels, they all disappeared down a pale green corridor. Allison started to follow but Grace stopped her.

"They'll take care of him, Allison. Now comes the really hard part." Her arm tightened around Allison's shoulders. "The waiting . . ."

Grace led them to a tiny room with hard wooden chairs designated for family and friends of patients. "Allison, sit down. You look like you're about to go into shock. Put your head between your legs, and I'll find you some tea or something."

Allison sunk into the chair and put her face in her hands. "Why does nothing ever turn out right in my life?" she muttered out loud. "Just when I find happiness, it's snatched away. Is my life cursed?"

A hand touched her shoulder and she looked up—there was Andrew. She threw herself into his arms and sobbed until no more tears would come. She stepped back in embarrassment, but his face was wet, too.

He handed her his handkerchief. "I don't know why these things happen. But somehow I believe everything will be okay."

She attempted a feeble smile and wiped her nose. "Thanks, Andrew."

Grace and Muriel came with tea for everyone. Allison's cry had cleared her head a bit. She looked over at Muriel's sad face and realized how much Grandpa must mean to her. After all, Muriel had known him for over thirty years, while she had only known him briefly. She wished she'd known Grandpa all her life. If only Marsha hadn't kept her away all these years. . . .

Grace left to see how he was doing. When she returned, Allison knew by her face the news wasn't good.

"He's pretty much the same. Dr. Hartley says it doesn't look very positive," Grace announced in a monotone voice, her face pale and expressionless.

"May I see him?" Allison asked.

"I don't know." Grace's eyes filled up, and Andrew stood once again to absorb Grace's tears as she cried on his shoulder.

Why? Why? Why? Allison wondered as she paced back and forth down the narrow corridor. The click of her heels on the shiny tile floor sounded hollow and empty, as if echoing the cries of her heart.

"I'll find out if you can see him," Grace offered as she wiped her eyes. Allison followed her to the nurses' station and waited as Grace spoke quietly to a large woman with steel gray hair and heavy-rimmed glasses. The woman frowned, glanced at her watch, then down at the clipboard on the counter.

"I guess it would be all right, but only a few minutes." She nodded to Allison.

Grace showed her to Grandpa's room. "I'll wait right here."

Allison hesitantly entered the dark room. Machines droned quietly and a bluish light illuminated the shiny, clear oxygen tent. It enveloped the bed like a shroud. Tubes protruded from Grandpa's nose, and his face was pale and lifeless. His chest moved steadily up and down in labored breathing. She slid her hand under the edge of the tent, grasped his hand, and lovingly stroked his callused fingers.

"Please don't leave me, Grandpa," she whispered. She stood motionless, gazing at his face—willing him to live.

A hand tapped her shoulder. "Allison," Grace whispered. "It's been ten minutes. We need go." To Allison it had felt like ten seconds, but she reluctantly followed Grace from the room.

"You know, Grace, you and Andrew should go home and get some rest," Allison suggested.

"Yes," Muriel agreed. "And you should take Allison with you. She's had a rough night, what with her swim in the inlet and all. I'm afraid she'll be sick next."

"I will not go home," Allison declared stubbornly.

"I couldn't sleep anyway," Grace added.

Andrew nodded. "And Heather and Winston are quite able to take care of things. . . ."

Allison walked down the hallway and stood at the long, narrow window. The sun was just coming over the hill and the sky was a deep, rosy shade of pink. Allison remembered the red sunset last night and her discussion with Grandpa about the sailor's warning. Was it only last night? It seemed a lifetime ago.

"Would you like some coffee, dear?" Grace asked from behind.

Allison spun around and exploded. "What was Grandpa doing out there in the middle of the night?" Grace jumped in surprise and splashed the scalding hot coffee on her fingers.

"Oh, I'm so sorry, Grace. Here, let me help you," Allison apologized, wiping the coffee from Grace's hand. "It's just that it hit me just now—why was Grandpa out in a boat at two in the morning?"

"I must admit, Allison, I wondered the same thing. I have absolutely no idea. Only Riley could tell you that." She sipped her coffee and looked out the window. "I just spoke with Dr. Hartley—no improvement, no change . . . I really think you should go home and rest. Muriel told me about the telegram last night. On top of everything else, I'm afraid you're going to wear yourself out. We need to take care of you for Riley's sake. You must realize that he could be here for days—"

"No, really, Grace, I'm fine. Please don't make me leave yet. I couldn't bear it."

Grace put her arm around her. "Allison, I don't claim to have all the answers, but I must tell you this. Every time I've gone through a trial I've tried to trust God, and in the end things always work out. Oh, maybe not like we expect; but they do work out."

Allison remembered Andrew's words. They had both said the same thing. Maybe that meant they were right. Maybe that meant Grandpa would be okay.

"Allison," Dr. Hartley approached them. "Your grandfather has regained consciousness. He wants to see you—but you must only stay briefly. He's extremely weak and not out of the woods yet."

Allison hugged Grace and dashed down the hall to Grandpa's room. She entered quietly and stood by his bed. Everything looked just as before, except that she noticed his eyelids flutter ever so slightly. Then they opened. Allison looked into his gray-blue eyes and a speck of hope crept into her heart like a warm ember. Drawing closer, she reached for his hand.

"Allison," he whispered. "Thank you."

"For what, Grandpa?"

"For coming to me . . . for bringing the letter . . ."

She could see speaking was difficult for him, and she felt torn between her desire to hear his words and wanting him to save his strength. But he was an O'Brian and, as Muriel so often pointed out, was bound to do as he liked.

"You gave me back my Jamie, Allison. I've been such a fool. . . ."

Allison shook her head as tears filled her eyes. "No, Grandpa, you're not a fool—"

"It doesn't matter anymore. I've forgiven him. That's all that matters. Now everything will be okay. . . ." He smiled and Allison's heart grew warmer. She could think of no words to say, but she held his hand and attempted to pour all her love down through her arm like a funnel into Grandpa. Soon the gray-haired nurse came in and nudged her.

"I love you, Grandpa, more than anyone in the whole world. I love you. See you later." He smiled and the nurse gently pulled her away. Allison released her grasp on his fingers, and he peacefully closed his eyes.

"How's he doing?" Muriel asked in the waiting room. Grace and Andrew listened anxiously.

"He's much better," Allison said. "He even talked to me."

"That's wonderful," Muriel replied. "I think we should go get a bite to eat before one of us needs a hospital bed. I can guarantee the cafeteria food is lousy, but there's a cafe down the street. I'll let them know at the front desk where we'll be in case they need to call us."

The little cafe felt cozy and cheerful compared to the sterile environment of the hospital. Allison took a deep breath and attempted to relax in the padded booth. She felt tired to the bone but at the same time energized by the hope that Grandpa was getting well. They all ordered hearty breakfasts, but no one had much of an appetite.

"I just know he's going to be better," Allison stated.

"Me too, darling," Muriel agreed.

She attempted to put a few bites of her breakfast into her mouth, but her stomach rebelled. "I'm ready to go back now," she announced, pushing an almost full plate toward the center of the table.

"I'll go with you," Andrew offered. He finished a strip of bacon and escorted Allison across the street.

"I really think you and Grace were right, Andrew. I'm just certain Grandpa is going to be all right and everything will work out in the end." She even ventured a feeble smile.

Dr. Hartley met them at the big swinging door. His eyes were sad. "Where are Grace and Muriel?" he asked, and Allison heard his voice catch. Andrew nodded wordlessly to the cafe across the street. Dr. Hartley took Allison gently by the arm and led her back across the street.

No! Allison screamed in her mind. Her ears started to ring, and the street looked all fuzzy. She saw Grace and Muriel, but they were fuzzy, too. Muriel rushed toward them.

"What is it, Dr. Hartley?"

"Riley's gone," he stated. "There was nothing more we could do. You knew it was just a matter of time. . . ."

Allison shook her head, trying to comprehend his meaning, but everything blurred—spun—faded into darkness. . . .

Fifteen

A STRANGE LIGHT FILTERED through the curtains. Allison rubbed her eyes and looked around. She was in her own room, and the sweet rosebuds smiled happily on the wallpaper. What time was it? Her clock said it wasn't quite eight, but it didn't feel like morning. Allison looked out her window to see dark clouds fill the sky. Maybe this was all just a horrible nightmare. Maybe Grandpa was downstairs in the dining room, just waiting for her to join him for breakfast. . . .

But there her suitcases stood by the door, packed and ready to go. The last few days blurred in her mind, partly due to those little yellow pills Dr. Hartley had prescribed and partly because she didn't want to face the truth. She clenched her teeth and forced herself to remember yesterday. The funeral at the stone church. The foggy cemetery on the hill. The three smooth gravestones, two old . . . one new. Grandpa was dead. She tried to convince herself with blunt cruelty. And today Lola would take her back—back to New York and crummy Camp Wannatonka. Her life was over. Everything she'd hoped for had died with Grandpa.

She wandered down the deserted hallway, her bare feet silent on the polished wood floor. The house felt sad . . . all of its family were dead. Even she felt dead. At the end of the hall, she leaned her head against the door with a hollow thud. End of the line. Again and again she bumped her head against the closed door. Maybe she could pound out the pain inside her heart. Her tears had dried up long ago. Finally the door gave in to her buffeting and lurched open, and she stumbled headfirst into what she'd assumed was merely a closet. Instead, it was a steep, narrow stairway that led up. As if in a trance, she followed the stairs that led to a closed door at the top.

The tarnished brass knob squeaked when she turned it, and Allison entered a small, round room. This would be the turret room. She'd never been up here before. She looked around without any real interest. Most of the furniture was draped in white dust cloths, and stacks of dusty paintings and empty canvases lined the walls. *This must've been my father's room*, she thought with only a faint trace of curiosity.

She absently browsed through the room's contents, unveiling furniture and examining unfinished seascapes and sketches. She held a small painting of the Jenson Lighthouse in her hands. It looked very real. He'd been a good artist, but where had it gotten him?

"Why have you all left me?" she screamed. She threw the unfinished painting to the floor, then swooped up a sketch pad and hurled it across the room. In a rage, she attacked the desk, scattering pens and paper, then yanked drawers out one by one and flung them to the floor. The last drawer stuck. She jerked and tugged and finally dropped to the floor in complete hopeless frustration.

Still clinging to the stubborn drawer, she sobbed again and again, "I wish I were dead, too! I wish I were dead, too!"

At last her tears subsided, and she wiped her face with her dusty hands. Something wedged in the drawer caught her eye, and she slid her hand down to dislodge an old plush box. It was identical to Marsha's. She opened it and the familiar, haunting strains of *Swan Lake* escaped. Inside the box nested dozens of letters, folded flat and smooth and tied with a ribbon. All were addressed to Mercury O'Brian, and they were all from Allison's father, James O'Brian. She opened the one on top.

December 16, 1932
Dear Mother,
    This isn't much of a Christmas present, but you know how it goes with us poor struggling artists. To be honest, I

found it at the five-and-dime, but I know how you love Swan
Lake—*it reminded me of you. I hope you have a Merry
Christmas. I only wish I could be there. It's going well here.
I've got six paintings showing in a very elite gallery on Fifth
Avenue. Hopefully one will sell any day now. I haven't heard
from Grace for months. Do you think she gave up on me? I
guess I can't blame her . . . she deserves better. I did meet an
interesting girl last week at the gallery. Her name is Marsha.
She's an actress and very beautiful but not my Grace. . . .*

> *All my love,*
> *James*

Allison quickly opened another.

February 19, 1933
Dear Mother,
    *I know this will shock you. Frankly it even shocks me. I
don't know what got into me. Maybe I was so overcome due
to the first sale of a painting. Maybe I was enchanted.*
    *The fact of the matter is, I married Marsha last weekend.
We just drove over to Jersey and tied the knot. I hope you'll
forgive me for not letting you see her first. I want to drive out
next summer and let you meet her. She's quite a gal.*

> *All my love,*
> *James*

Allison considered his words. It didn't sound like he even
loved Marsha. Why did he marry her? Was it just because he
thought he'd lost Grace? She quickly opened another letter in
the stack and sucked in her breath. It was dated on her birthday.

January 24, 1934
Dear Mother,
    *Congratulations, Grandmother! (I can't imagine you as a
grandmother. You're too pretty.) Today we had a baby girl, Al-*

lison Mercury O'Brian, seven pounds, two ounces. (Marsha
said I misspelled Allison, but I like it with two l's.) She's all
red and wrinkly, but when I saw her for the first time I fell
in love. I held her for a couple of hours before the nurses
caught on and snatched her away. Marsha's father helped me
to get a job with National Insurance of New York. Since I'm
a daddy now, I've decided to put away the paint box and do
the nine-to-five routine like the rest of the civilized world.
Marsha isn't too thrilled about being a mother. I thought she'd
be happy, but her career is just picking up. Anyway, your
granddaughter is a sweetie. Please ask Father to write . . . he
never answers my letters.

> All my love,
> James

The next few letters were short and dreary. Her father, obviously trapped in a sour marriage, tried to keep Marsha happy.
But all she cared about was her career. He complained about
his in-laws, who'd practically stolen his child, but his hands
seemed tied. She opened the next letter.

December 11, 1941
Dear Mother,

This is my blackest month. I hate to worry you, but our
correspondence has been my only comfort. Just two days after
the devastating news of Pearl Harbor, I received a bombshell
of my own. I've been accused of embezzlement in the insurance corporation. What a cruel joke! I barely have two coins
to rub together and my "wife" makes more than me. That
brings me to another subject. We're separated now. I don't
want a divorce, if only for the sake of Allison. My mother-in-
law never lets me see her as it is. I know her excuses are mostly
lies, and I strongly suspect she may be behind this whole embezzlement scheme. If I can get the evidence I need, it will
clear my name and possibly win Allison back to me. If not, I

may just join the army and throw myself full force into the war effort. If you can think of anything to help dear Allison, please do it.

> *All my love,*
> *James*

The next letters were written on V-mail, the kind servicemen used during the war. The one she held in her hands was dated in June of 1942.

Dear Mother,

Your idea about having Allison visit is just super. I only hope you can swing it. Mrs. Madison can be about as friendly as a Hun. But if anyone can sweet-talk her, it's you. Good luck! I've written Marsha several times, but all I've received is a card with an autographed pinup photo. The guys don't believe she's really my wife. She's quite a hit these days. I'm hoping she'll get Hollywood out of her system after the war and want to be a mother to Allison and a wife to me. The battlefield can really change a guy's outlook.

> *All my love,*
> *James*

Allison's heart ached for the lonely G.I. on the battlefront, longing for his sweetheart and not knowing his days were numbered. The next letter remained unopened. She felt certain it must've come after Grandmother's death. It was dated in September, and it was depressing and gloomy and almost too painful to read.

Dear Mother,

You've been my one bright and shining light through this mess, and I thank you for it. If I never make it out of here alive, I won't be sorry. My only regrets are the way I've disappointed you and Father, and not being able to be a daddy to Allison. *The divorce is final. . . . Marsha has custody of the child she never wanted. My reputation remains in ruins, as you and Father have been made painfully aware. I heard Grace married a wonderful man. I'm happy for her. If only I hadn't been such a fool. No second chances for me, though. . . .*

> *All my love,*
> *James*

Life was black for him then. *Just like it is for me now,* Allison thought. She knew her father had died the following month. It had been carved into her memory—October 1942.

Yet there were still some letters in Grandmother's box. She pulled out the last three, all unopened. She quickly scanned them and her heart pounded in her ears. They were all from overseas—and they were all from James O'Brian! The first two described more horrors of war. One dated December 1943—the next, February 1944. She opened the last, dated in November 1944. How could this be? She read it in wonder.

Dear Mother,

I don't blame you for not writing, though it's not like you. I'm in an army hospital in England. Don't be alarmed. I'm okay, just a little beat up. They'll be shipping me home as soon as I'm able. I've begged them to let me stay and return to the front, but they say I'm unfit. Unfit to be killed? Interesting. But I must admit it will be nice to see you. I want to come home to Oregon first. I only hope Father will speak to me again and allow me to stay at least until I recover. All I need is peace and quiet and a place to paint.

> *All my love,*
> *James*

"He's not dead!" Allison gasped. "*He's not dead!*" She rose from the rubble on the floor and stretched her cramped legs.

Still in her nightgown, she shivered as she paced the room. "Where can he be?" she asked the empty room. "Where is he now?" She felt as if she stood on the abyss in her dream, about to tumble into a pit of insanity. She drew open the dusty drapes to reveal a band of windows that encased the room. Beyond them, the most spectacular view from the house was exposed— every direction for as far as the eye could see. Heavy black clouds piled up on the ocean, and the sky had an odd greenish cast.

Out the north window stood the Jenson Light, its beam shining proudly. Perhaps the only remnant of stability left to this family.

"The mad lighthouse keeper!" she exclaimed. "Grandpa— the rowboat—he was on his way to the lighthouse!"

Allison dashed down the narrow staircase and into her room. She jerked on warm clothes right over her nightgown and tore down the stairs.

The sky was dark and angry, and the waves had sharp white-caps. She didn't check the tide—it made no difference. The little boat clanked hard against the dock as it was pitched by the waves. She struggled to untie it and began to row for the lighthouse. She felt Grandpa in the oars. His hands had grasped them only a few nights ago, but his failing heart had aborted his mission. She would finish it now.

The storm came on fast. Raindrops like tiny daggers were driven by the wind and pierced her face. The waves grew tall and menacing. She fixed her eyes on the light and rowed furi-ously toward it. As the boat dove deep into the well of each wave, the lighthouse vanished, and she wondered if she'd be devoured by the sea. It didn't matter, though, for she felt no fear—only a driving force to find her father.

At last Allison saw the light towering directly overhead. The next instant the rowboat smashed onto the rocks, and the force of the impact thrust her into the pounding surf. She kicked and fought to cling to the rocks and extract herself from the ocean's mighty grip. The boat was gone.

The jagged rocks cut into her hands like knives as she struggled to crawl up. Even on the flat shore of the island, huge, fierce breakers beat down upon her and pummeled her body into the ground. She flattened herself on the rocks near the lighthouse, clinging for life. *God, help me,* she cried.

When she finally reached the shelter of the lighthouse, an immense wave washed over the whole island and tried to sweep her away. She clung to the wet surface of the building, digging in with her fingernails until the wave died down, then she worked her way around to the door, leaving a trail of blood from her own hands along the white walls.

The heavy wooden door was bolted tight. Desperate, she pounded and yelled with the last of her strength, but her screams were swallowed by the wailing storm. A large brass ring served as a door pull, and she wrapped her fingers around its encrusted surface.

The door faced east, slightly protected from the full force of the storm. Pounding and screaming were pointless. She was a fool—just like her father. He probably wasn't even here. With bitter irony she figured there probably was a mad lighthouse keeper and perhaps her father really was dead. Allison's head reeled, and her grip on the ring loosened as she slipped into oblivion.

Sixteen

SHE WAS A LITTLE GIRL AGAIN, hiding under Nanny Jane's crisp white apron, and the light shone through and smelled as sweet as sunshine. But something was tickling her nose. Allison awoke wrapped in a scratchy woolen quilt with a fat tortoiseshell cat snuggled up next to her face. A fire burned in a potbellied stove, and an odd smell filled the air. Turpentine?

Sitting across from her—waiting expectantly—was a man who could have passed for Vincent VanGogh, or perhaps her father. His auburn hair and beard stuck out in wild woolly tufts, and his nose had a streak of black across it.

"Here." He held a mug of tea in front of her. "Don't try to talk yet. Just drink this." She obeyed, not daring to take her eyes off of him lest he disappear—like a mirage. His brow furrowed deeply as he stared at her with equal intensity.

"I can't take it any longer!" The words exploded from his mouth, and Allison drew back in fear. He stood for a moment, paced back and forth like a caged lion, and continued, "Could you—is it possible? Are you my daughter? Are you my Allison Mercury? Or have I completely lost my senses as they all claim?"

Allison broke into a tiny smile. "No, you're not mad. I am Allison . . . and I think you're my father."

With a massive sigh, he rushed to her and swooped her up as if she were a small child. As he held her, Allison felt the strength in his arms and knew she was in good hands.

"What could have possessed you to pull such a stunt?" he asked suddenly, holding her at arm's length. "What were you thinking to take a boat out in this weather? You could have been killed." He placed her gently back in the chair and tucked the blanket around her. Then he ran his fingers through his untamed hair and continued in a calmer voice. "I'm sorry. . . . I'm not angry with you. I just can't understand what you were thinking. If it hadn't been for Picasso"—he pointed at the cat—"I probably never would've found you."

Allison stroked the cat now purring contentedly in her lap. She didn't know what to say. Instead, she just stared as her father rubbed his whiskers and paced across the tiny room, talking as he went.

"Picasso slipped out right before the storm and I was watching for him, but instead I found a half-drowned maiden on my doorstep. It isn't that I'm not delighted to see you, Allison. I'm overcome with joy. But you took such a risk! What if—" He stared at her in wonder.

"It's a long story, Dad," she said slowly with a sigh. It felt good to call him Dad. She watched him retrieve a pipe from a crude wooden shelf above the wood stove. He shook it out and refilled it with fresh tobacco. Taking his time, he packed it carefully. He glanced out at the storm still raging.

"We've got all the time in the world." He lit his pipe and leaned back in his chair, never moving his gaze from her.

Allison looked down at Picasso and wondered where she should begin. She told him about her childhood and Nanny Jane.

"Well, I thank God for dear Mrs. McAllister," James said. "She wrote me occasionally and told me how you were doing. As badly as I wanted you with me, I knew you were better off with her than with Marsha—I'm sorry to tell you that, Allison."

She nodded. She above anyone else understood this. Then she told him about boarding school and Patricia and Miss Snyder, explaining the summer camp dilemma and her escape across the country. When she got to the part about Grandpa, her voice broke into sobs and her father's face paled.

"I loved him so much. Why did he have to die?" She looked up to see her father's face contorted in pain as silent tears slid down his cheeks. Then he buried his head in his hands and sobbed. Allison's pain seemed to diminish slightly as she tried to comfort her father. She stood by his side and placed her hand on his shoulder.

"He said he forgives you, Dad," she said softly.

He looked at her with a creased brow and shook his head in disbelief. "Really? He did?"

She shook him gently for emphasis. "In the hospital—those were his last words." She sunk into the chair, weak and fatigued from her fight against the storm. She sipped her lukewarm tea. "Oh yes, I almost forgot. I found a letter at Marsha's. It was written by some guy . . . Hardwick. It was meant to clear your name about the embezzlement scandal, I guess. I suppose Marsha never sent it to you."

He stood and his eyes blazed. "I should have known!"

"So is that why you have been hiding out here? Why everyone thought you were dead? Even me?"

He shook his head. "I'm sorry, Allison. But there just didn't seem to be any other way. It was your grandfather's idea at first. I got pretty shot up in the war. And after I was released from the hospital, I came back home to recover. But I still had that crazy embezzlement charge over my head, and he thought I should come out here to stay until I figured out a way to prove my innocence and clear my name. I came to like it out here. I started painting, and it helped me to forget the war and the pain of a failed marriage—and the loss of you."

"So you were just going to stay here forever?" Allison asked. "Would I have ever gotten to know you?"

James shook his head. "Believe me, I planned and dreamed about how I would get you back. But eventually I began to wonder if my plans were just selfish. I assumed you had a great life and didn't need me butting in. You had wealthy grandparents, a wonderful nanny, and a movie star for a mother. What could I give you? Besides, I figured that they had all poisoned your mind against me, and if I tried to get you back, I would probably end up in prison. I finally just gave up."

"I see your point," Allison muttered. "It's just so unfair. I can't believe Marsha kept us apart all this time—and kept that letter from you."

"It's not all Marsha's fault. Her mother had her very well trained." He looked at Allison apologetically. "I'm sorry, I shouldn't talk about your mother and your grandmother like that. I have made it my life goal to forgive them both, but God has to help me more than most. Still, I wouldn't be surprised if Marsha's mother had told her to burn that letter."

"We can be glad that she didn't burn it, because when I showed it to Grandpa, he realized you were innocent. I think that's why he tried to take out the rowboat—to come here and tell you. I think he figured with that letter, you might be able to help me—oh, I almost forgot! Marsha's lawyer wired that I must return. In fact, Lola is coming out here to pick me up." She smiled faintly, imagining Lola's face to find her gone.

"Over my dead body!" He stood tall, feet straddled and arms folded across his chest—a formidable foe.

Allison sighed. She felt safe and at home. Tiny as the lighthouse might be, she'd be content to stay as long as her father was there. "We could just hide out here in the lighthouse," she suggested.

He paced once again and puffed on his pipe. The smoke smelled sweet, almost fruity—nothing like Stanley's stale cigars. His old gray woolen shirt was a collage of multicolored paint splotches. It resembled some modern art Allison had seen in a city gallery once. She glanced around the room and noticed the stacks of finished paintings that lined the walls. There were seascapes, fishing boats, lighthouses, still lifes, and even some impressionistic works. It was obvious he'd made good use of his time during those seemingly wasted years.

"No, I don't think we'll continue to be fugitives, Allison. Not that I'd mind so much, but think about George and Muriel. They'll be worried sick—"

"And there's Grace and the Amberwells," Allison exclaimed. "I almost forgot."

"Grace? Amberwells?" her father questioned with a puzzled expression. Allison's eyes lit up in remembrance of Grace's story about the lost romance.

"Yes, Grace. She happens to be one of the nicest women I've ever met. And the Amberwells are the orphans she brought back from England. There's Heather and Winston and Andrew—"

"But what about Grace?"

"Well, she lives on the other side of the bluff with these kids. And she's been a good friend to me. She even told me all about her first sweetheart—how she believed in him and waited . . ." James slumped into his chair with his head bowed down. She felt guilty for tormenting him so, but she was relieved to see that he still cared.

"And did she tell you what a fool I was?"

"Well, speaking from experience, it seems to run in our family," Allison chided in an attempt at lightness.

"So it's Grace Amberwell now. How is her husband?"

"No, her name's not Amberwell. Her husband was shot down over France right after they were married. Then she adopted the Amberwell children because their parents died in the London bombings. It's kind of a long story, but if I were you, I wouldn't waste any time. Reverend Simmons is awfully nice, and he's been making sheep's eyes at Grace."

James shook his head slowly and stared at Allison as if she were delirious. "You mentioned that letter—do you still have it?"

"I gave it to Grandpa." She looked down at Picasso and traced her finger over the crazy patterns of his odd-colored coat.

"It's probably still on his desk. He was going to send it to his lawyer—"

"Just what I was thinking. That letter will most likely verify my innocence—maybe I can even use it to force Marsha into relinquishing your custody." He pulled back a wooden shutter and peered out the thick glass of the tiny porthole window. "Still awful out there—worst squall I've seen in some time. Good thing this lighthouse is built like a rock. I've got some stew on the stove, and you look like you could use some."

Allison nodded, feeling hungry for the first time in days. She glanced at her wrist. Her hands were cut and bruised, and her watch face was smashed. "What time is it?"

"Half past five," he answered. "You slept most of the day." He handed her a heaping bowl of stew. "There's no way we'll make it out tonight. For once I almost wish I had a telephone or shortwave. I've always liked my isolation here. It's like a giant cloak of protection. And between you and me, I used to fuel those mad lighthouse keeper stories. If anyone came snooping around in a boat, I'd pull a stocking cap on my head and dash out with paint on my face and screech and howl at them." He chuckled. "It was a good form of entertainment."

"How long have you been here?" Allison asked, blowing on a spoonful of stew.

"Well, it was winter of '44 when I came home. I really took your grandfather by surprise. He'd never even opened my letters after Mother died. He just stashed them away. You see, he blamed me for Mother's death. Maybe he was partly right. . . ."

Allison shook her head, but he continued.

"I was already a mess, and to find out about her was almost more than I could bear. My father had already been having trouble with the government lighthouse keeper—drinking and not keeping the light running right. So he got permission to sack him and put me in as a temporary replacement. It was actually kind of interesting during the war. I used to have to watch for

Japanese aircraft and ships and subs. I had a shortwave back then. But temporary soon became permanent, and this is home for me now. George is the only person besides your grandfather who knows I'm here. He brings me supplies every Sunday, weather permitting.

"Now I think of all the years I've wasted—all because of that trumped-up embezzlement charge. If only I'd known about that letter!" He slammed his fist onto the table with such force, his empty cup crashed to the floor. "I'm sorry, Allison. It's just so frustrating."

"I understand. When I think of the lost years I didn't even know I had a father or a grandpa . . . I guess I should just be thankful to have known Grandpa for the short time I did." She tried to swallow the lump in her throat. "Without Grandpa, I wouldn't have found you."

His smile lit up his face and warmed her heart. "As for you, my dear Allison, you need some sleep. You've been through a rough week. Finish up that stew, and then we'll get you off to bed."

As much as she wanted to stay up and talk, she couldn't argue. Her body cried for rest.

James tucked her into the narrow bunk built right into the thick plastered wall. He pulled the woolly blankets up to her chin and leaned over to kiss her good-night. Tears of happiness filled her eyes, and his scratchy whiskers didn't bother her a bit.

"Where will you sleep?" she asked groggily.

"Don't you worry about me. I'm too worked up to sleep and I've got a lot to do. Just sleep, dear Allison," he whispered as he turned down the kerosene wick.

∞ ∞ ∞

The smell of oatmeal roused her senses, and Allison opened her eyes to see the sun shining brightly through the salt-encrusted porthole window. A heaping bowl of oatmeal sat on a roughhewn table with a mug of tea beside it. Her clothes were cleaned and dried, and her torn trouser knees had been mended. She hungrily devoured the oatmeal and tea, but where was her father?

She glanced at the cuckoo clock on the wall—it was almost noon. How in the world did she sleep so long? Her body felt stiff and sore. Ugly bruises and scrapes covered her arms and legs. She dressed slowly. *I feel like I've been run over by a truck,* she thought. But for the first time in the last few days her heart felt lighter.

She made her way down to the rocks, where she saw a neatly attired man stacking boxes beside a large rowboat. A second glance told her it was her father.

"What happened to your beard?" she asked, studying his handsome, clean-shaven face in amazement. His hair was combed and trimmed and he looked ten years younger. He still had that rugged outdoorsman look, only now in a more dignified way. "You look great, Dad!"

"Thanks. It's terrific to hear you call me Dad. I'm almost ready to go—how about you? Did you eat your mush and find everything you need?"

Allison nodded as she slowly eased her aching body into the boat. She looked back up at the lighthouse, taking in each detail. "I always wanted to see this place close up," she remarked. The sky was clear blue and the ocean remarkably calm after yesterday's squall. Little waves lapped pleasantly on the rocks, making a happy, peaceful sound.

James glided the boat through the inlet. Allison admired his long, even strokes, and the boat sliced swiftly through the gently rolling waves.

"Hey, there's someone on the dock!" Allison exclaimed. She peered hard. "It's Andrew!"

She waved both arms frantically. As they drew closer, Andrew recognized her and he leaped up and down, waving and yelling at the top of his lungs. Before James could even dock the boat, Andrew reached over and pulled Allison out and hugged her hard.

"We thought you'd drowned! I found bits of the rowboat washed up—the Coast Guard's coming to search! And your mother's secretary has been out here looking for you. We gotta tell the folks!"

"Slow down, Andrew. Come meet my father, James O'Brian!" Andrew's eyes widened and his jaw dropped. Just then the others came running down the dock road.

"What is it, Andrew?" Grace screamed. "Did you find her?" Heather clung to Grace's arm, and the others followed on their heels.

Allison stepped into full view and waved. "I'm okay," she cried, running to meet them. "I'm so sorry I scared you all." She embraced Grace and Heather. Muriel, George, and Winston quickly joined the huddle. Everyone was laughing and crying all at once. Muriel even scolded Allison, and they all asked dozens of questions.

"I'll explain everything," Allison said. Then she added loud enough to get their attention, "But I had to find my dad!" Everyone ceased talking and looked at Allison in puzzlement. Suddenly, Grace's face grew deathly pale, and Allison watched her look toward Andrew still on the dock. James was next to him, tying up the boat.

"Jamie? No, it can't be!" shrieked Muriel. She clutched George's sleeve and shook her head in disbelief. But George nodded and smiled, wrapping his short arms around her.

"Your father is alive?" Heather questioned. "That's wonderful, Allison!" The two girls hugged in delight.

"I know I've got a lot of explaining to do," James began as he joined the bewildered crowd and exchanged hugs and greetings, "if you'll give me time. Let's all go up to the house and I'll tell you about it. I also have a plan for keeping Allison with us—always."

George carefully guided the joyous yet stunned Muriel up the hill, and Andrew slung Winston over his shoulder. The two whooped and galloped toward the house. Allison squeezed Heather's hand as she held her breath and watched her father standing humbly before Grace.

"Grace, I can't begin to tell you how sorry I am about everything that's passed between us. I've been a first-class fool, that's for sure. I'm just hoping somehow you'll find room in your heart to forgive me." He dropped his head, and Allison ached for him.

"Oh, James, you always did have the Irish gift of the Blarney, didn't you?" He looked up in surprise, and Grace smiled and reached out to firmly clasp his hand. Her face regained its color with even the faint glow of a blush.

Allison rushed over and vigorously hugged them both.

"Well, Dad," she said. "Seems you and I have taken the long way home."

"Yes," James replied, giving her another hug. "But it's sure great to be back."

❧   ❧   ❧

Allison's joyful reunion with her father is cut short when her mother insists Allison leave Oregon at once to spend the rest of her summer at camp. Things only get worse when her parents become involved in a fierce custody suit over her. Torn between her father's love and her mother's approval, Allison is caught in the middle. Can she trust herself to make the decision of a lifetime? Find out in *Cherished Wish*, THE ALLISON CHRONICLES #2.

Teen Series From
Bethany House Publishers

— ⨯⨯⨯ —

Early Teen Fiction (11–14)

THE ALLISON CHRONICLES by Melody Carlson
Follow along as Allison O'Brian, the daughter of a famous 1940s movie star, searches for the truth about her past and the love of a family.

HIGH HURDLES by Lauraine Snelling
Show jumper DJ Randall strives to defy the odds and achieve her dream of winning Olympic Gold.

SUMMERHILL SECRETS by Beverly Lewis
Fun-loving Merry Hanson encounters mystery and excitement in Pennsylvania's Amish country.

THE TIME NAVIGATORS by Gilbert Morris
Travel back in time with Danny and Dixie as they explore unforgettable moments in history.

Young Adult Fiction (12 and up)

CEDAR RIVER DAYDREAMS by Judy Baer
Experience the challenges and excitement of high school life with Lexi Leighton and her friends.

GOLDEN FILLY SERIES by Lauraine Snelling
Tricia Evanston races to become the first female jockey to win the sought-after Triple Crown.

JENNIE MCGRADY MYSTERIES by Patricia Rushford
A contemporary Nancy Drew, Jennie McGrady's sleuthing talents bring back readers again and again.

LIVE! FROM BRENTWOOD HIGH by Judy Baer
The staff of an action-packed teen-run news show explores the love, laughter, and tears of high school life.

THE SPECTRUM CHRONICLES by Thomas Locke
Adventure and romance await readers in this fantasy series set in another place and time.

SPRINGSONG BOOKS by various authors
Compelling love stories and contemporary themes promise to capture the hearts of readers.

WHITE DOVE ROMANCES by Yvonne Lehman
Romance, suspense, and fast-paced action for teens committed to finding pure love.